Tutankhamun's Book of Puzzles

METRO BOOKS
New York

An Imprint of Sterling Publishing
387 Park Avenue South
New York, NY 10016

METRO BOOKS and the distinctive Metro Books logo are trademarks of Sterling Publishing Co., Inc.

© 2013 by Carlton Books Ltd

This 2013 edition published by Metro Books by arrangement with Carlton Books Limited.

ISBN 978-1-4351-4899-4

For information about custom editions, special sales, and premium and corporate purchases, please contact Sterling Special Sales at 800-805-5489 or specialsales@sterlingpublishing.com.

Manufactured in China

2 4 6 8 10 9 7 5 3 1

www.sterlingpublishing.com

The copyright holders would like to thank the following sources for their kind permission to reproduce the pictures in this book.
Alamy: /Michal Boubin: 4, 25, 175; /Ivy Close Images: 54, 106, 192, 221; /Mary Evans Picture Library: 45, 77, 144; /Robert Harding Picture Library: 12, 148
iStockphoto.com: 8, 13, 16, 42, 46, 49, 50, 58, 60, 65, 76, 78, 86, 91, 92, 96, 112, 123, 132, 149, 153, 165, 166, 196, 207, 224, 247, 256
Photo12: /Ann Ronan Picture Library: 1, 3
Thinkstock: 6, 11, 17, 22, 27, 30, 32, 34, 36, 37, 41, 47, 48, 51, 55, 64, 68, 69, 70, 73, 80, 83, 90, 93, 99, 101, 104, 105, 107, 110, 114, 117, 124, 126, 128, 130, 131, 134, 137, 145, 146, 147, 150, 154, 158, 159, 162, 168, 171, 173, 174, 178, 180, 185, 188, 189, 193, 198, 201, 202, 204, 210, 218, 222, 226, 240, 245, 248, 251, 254, 255
Every effort has been made to acknowledge correctly and contact the source and or copyright holder of each picture and Carlton Books Limited apologises for any unintentional errors or omissions, which will be corrected in future editions of this book.

Tutankhamun's Book of Puzzles

RIDDLES & ENIGMAS
INSPIRED BY THE
GREAT PHARAOH

TIM DEDOPULOS

METRO BOOKS
New York

CONTENTS

AUTHOR'S NOTE

In compiling this book, I have taken some horrible liberties with Ancient Egyptian culture, and with history in general. Sorry. Where puzzles clashed with reality, puzzles had to win. I have done my best to stay true to mythology, locations, units, and other factors as much as possible. As the mythic aspects of Ancient Egypt did not generally cause problems with puzzle design, I believe most of it to be at least broadly accurate. I hope so, anyway. Other aspects, however, did not do as well. In particular, any links I have made between puzzles and specific places are purely imaginary. So please, take the historical content with a pinch of salt; I hope you enjoy the puzzles.

Tim Dedopulos, *May 2012.*

INTRODUCTION

MIGHTY TUTANKHAMUN, LORD OF THE FORMS OF RE, HE WHO WEARS the Crowns of his Father, Strong Bull who is Pleasing of Birth, Greatest of the Palace of Amun, Ruler of All, your name shall surely echo down through the aeons into the most distant futures. May you be remembered even when the world is old, and man dreams strange and impossible dreams. The wisdom and beauty of your rule will live on, and even thousands of years hence, your august name will be synonymous with the splendour and might of our beloved Egypt. I know this to be true. I have seen it.

Ever your humble servant, I have obeyed your command, and prepared for your edification and amusement a scroll of all manner of puzzles and problems. I have scoured the wisdom of the civilied lands – yea, and even beyond – to compile questions which may bring you some small satisfaction. Some embody certain curious circumstances that I have come to learn of. A few matters are even of direct practical concern. Others are entirely abstract, belonging purely to the realms of Seshat, and if there is any enlightenment herein, it surely comes from She Who Scribes, and not from my unworthy quill.

I have endeavoured to make the terms of each problem as clear as I am able. If there is any uncertainty involved, it comes from my own lamentable failings. The puzzles are structured in such a way as to collect the simpler ones towards the beginning of the scroll, the more complex ones towards the end, and those of middling difficulty in the middle. Solutions to each question can be found at the finish of the document, in the same order as the problems they answer. I pray most fervently that all is to your satisfaction, my lord.

Tutankhamun, best-loved of all the Pharaohs of Egypt throughout time, I salute you.

EASY
PUZZLES

In this first section, my Pharaoh, the problems that you will encounter are the ones that appeared to me to be reasonably simple. Although your mighty wisdom knows no restraints, and all such earthly trials must seem to you as the machinations of young children, it seemed to me that mere mortals might prefer a lesser challenge in the beginning.

PROBLEM 1

I N THE CITY OF SARDES, THE DOCKSIDE STORAGE AREA IS arranged in a curious manner that makes theft easier to spot.

Crates of goods are stored in a grid, seven piles long and seven piles wide. No pile is ever left empty, nor is any loaded more than seven crates high. In each row and in each column there is exactly one pile of each height, no more, no less.

Some piles are required to be higher than a neighbouring pile, these are indicated by an arrow which points to the lower pile.

From the sketch I have drawn here, can you calculate the number of crates on each pile of the grid?

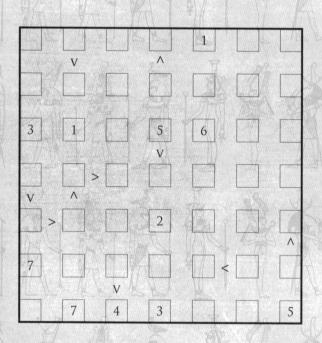

solution on page 167

PROBLEM 2

THREE LOAVES OF BREAD ARE TO BE DIVIDED BETWEEN FIVE labourers. Each man must get pieces of identical size to his fellow workers, and no man may receive more than one piece of the same size. How would you divide the bread?

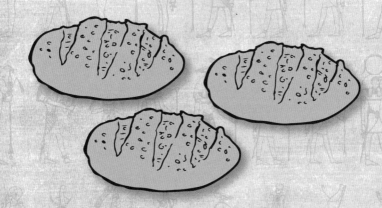

Solution on page 168

PROBLEM 3

H AVE YOU EVER WONDERED WHAT MAKES A GOOD GAME? I suggest that a good game must have both an element of strategy and an element of chance. A better player should be able to beat a lesser, but this should not be absolute. So consider the well-known child's game which uses a grid of three squares by three. Two players take turns to make their mark on an empty square, and win by filling a clear line of three squares before their opponent. Do I consider this a good game?

Solution on page 169

PROBLEM 4

❖

I BEG YOU, STRONG BULL, TURN YOUR MIND TO THIS TRIFLING issue. At a certain time of day, a pole that is 1 metre tall casts a shadow of 75cm. At the same time, there is a tree whose shadow is 8 metres long. How tall is it?

Solution on page 169

PROBLEM 5

H ERE ARE TWO SETS OF MATHEMATICAL OPERATIONS, WITH their answers. The digits have been replaced by symbols, which are consistent in both sets. What is the missing number?

$$\text{🜪 🐏 🜩} \times$$
$$\text{👁 🐏}$$

$$= \text{⛩ 🦁 🦁 👁 👁} +$$
$$\text{👁 👁 👁 🐏 🦁}$$

$$= 3 \quad 8 \quad 2 \quad 5 \quad 8$$

$$\text{👁 🦅 🧍} \times$$
$$\text{? \quad ?}$$

$$= \text{⛩ ⛩ 👁 👁 🧍} +$$
$$\text{🐏 ⭕ 👁 🦆 ⛩}$$

$$= 4 \quad 8 \quad 1 \quad 1 \quad 6$$

✦ Solution on page 108 ✦

PROBLEM 6

———◆———

I HAVE AN INTERESTING LITTLE DIVERSION THAT IS SUPPOSED to have originated in Mycenae. In the grid below is a selection of paired tiles. Each pair must be connected by an unbroken path of tiles that can travel both horizontally and vertically. No two paths can cross. No path forms a loop, not even a closed knot of a square of four touching cells. One square, indicated by a star, does not form part of the pattern; all the rest are taken up by the paths of tiles. Can you uncover them?

Solution on page 170

PROBLEM 7

L ORD OF ALL, IN THIS PROBLEM, THREE PAIRS OF NUMBERS are connected through a mathematical operation to a common answer. What is the missing number?

Solution on page 171

PROBLEM 8

A ROYAL CHARIOT ARCHER CAN FIRE 8 ARROWS PER MINUTE and hit his target two fifths of the time.

A Nile bowman can fire 6 arrows per minute and find his mark a third of the time.

On the battlefield a group of 15 chariot archers and a group of 25 bowmen prepare to fire. Which group will hit the most targets in the next minute?

Solution on page 171

PROBLEM 9

THESE BOARDS ARE TO BE COMBINED INTO ONE SUMMARY board, but they do so in a curious fashion. If a dark square is present on an odd number of boards, it is present in the summary, but if it is coloured on an even number of boards, it is not shown. What does the summary board look like?

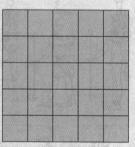

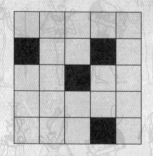

Solution on page 172

PROBLEM 10

❖

I N THE EQUATIONS SCRIBED BELOW, VARIOUS WHOLE NUMBERS have been replaced with glyphs. Assuming that for each equation, the calculations are performed strictly in the order they appear, what are the numbers?

$$\text{(seated figure)} + \text{(bull)} - \text{(bird)} = 1$$

$$\text{(bull)} \times \text{(seated figure)} + \text{(bird)} = 10$$

$$\text{(bird)} - \text{(seated figure)} + \text{(bull)} = 5$$

$$\text{(seated figure)} \times \text{(bird)} \times \text{(bull)} = 24$$

Solution on page 172

PROBLEM 11

T HE RIGHT-HAND TILE RELATES TO THE LEFT-HAND TILE in a consistent manner. What does the missing tile look like?

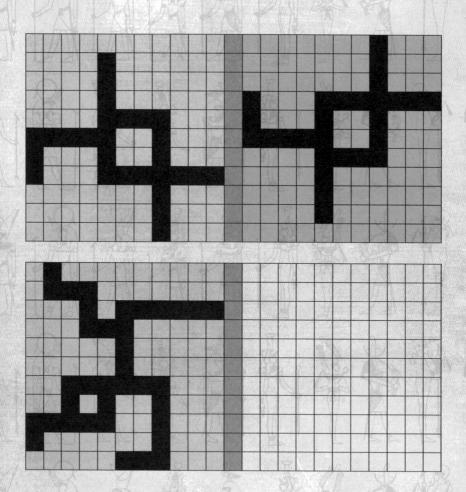

Solution on page 173

PROBLEM 12

———◆———

THIS BEAM IS IN BALANCE OVER THE PIVOT THAT IS SHOWN. You may assume that the beam and connecting rods are all perfectly stiff and counter-weight each other perfectly, and that the marked divisions are of identical length. What is the weight of the block bearing a question mark?

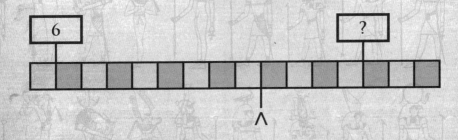

Solution on page 173

PROBLEM 13

A DOG SPOTS A HARE 50 CUBITS DISTANT, AND GIVES CHASE. The dog will catch the hare after 125 cubits, but when the distance between the two is just 30 cubits, how much further will the chase have to run?

Solution on page 174

PROBLEM 14

CONSIDER THESE NUMBERED GRIDS. EACH FOLLOWS ON FROM the one before. Where will the glyphs be in the fourth?

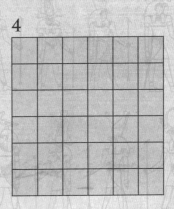

Solution on page 174

PROBLEM 15

Mastery of tactics depends in part on awareness of opportunity. Consider the field displayed here. Take each square to be a *khet* in length. Each number represents an archer stationed in the field. There are obstructions in the field, which are not shown. They are considered to occupy a single square each. Each archer is to be thought of as reporting the number of squares in the field that he can see, vertically or horizontally, including the square he is on. So a man reporting four squares is able to see his own space and just three others. Archers do not obstruct each other, and do not stand on obstructions. No two obstructions are in horizontal or vertical contact. Can you calculate the precise extent of each man's range?

								5		13	
		5				14					
7											
	12								5		
				12			12				4
	11		2						9		
		5							12	17	
8			8		13						
		10								11	
											7
				10				15			
	11		8								

Solution on page 175

PROBLEM 16

A FOOLISH MERCHANT HAS BEEN SELLING COUNTERFEIT ICONS of the Gods. Gathered here are a number of likenesses of Bastet, the protector. Two of the icons are genuine and perfect, but the other six all bear various flaws. Which are originals?

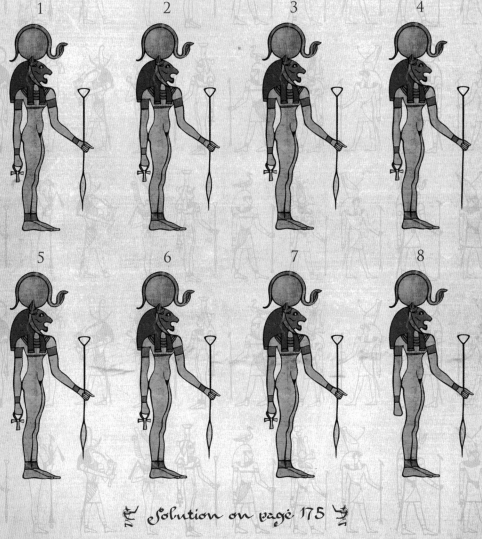

Solution on page 175

PROBLEM 17

THIS SQUARE OF NUMBERS IS A THING OF POTENT MAGIC. Its Heka is such that every row and column adds up to the same total, as do the two major diagonals. The pairs of numbers fit into the horizontal empty spots on the grid. What is the complete square?

		7		
		25		
17	5	13	21	9
		1		
		19		

14	22		23	6
4	12		10	18
20	3		2	15
11	24		8	16

Solution on page 176

PROBLEM 18

———— ◆ ————

Y OU WELL KNOW, MIGHTY PHARAOH, THAT WE DIVIDE OUR day into twenty-four hours. Perhaps Seshat has touched me with her wisdom, for I foresee that the day will come when every hour will be deemed to have the same length, and each will be split into sixty divisions, minutes, in the Sumerian way. If that is not enough to ponder, consider this. The time is 05:41. What time will it be when these four digits next describe the minute?

Solution on page 176

PROBLEM 19

—◆—

I N Aaru, the eternally living enjoy their reward for a blameless life. The reed-field islands are as numberless as they are lush and bountiful.

In this design, a dominion of islands is marked out. It is possible to get to any island from any other, as they are interlinked by either single or double pathways. The pathways are straight, horizontal and vertical, do not bend or cross each other, and terminate invariably at an island. Each island bears a tally of the total number of pathways touching it. Where do the paths fall?

	1		3			6			4
4					4				
	1			3		3		1	
					2				
	2			5		6			6
							1		
	2								
	1								
5						6		2	
							1		5
1		2		3		3		1	
						1			3

Solution on page 177

PROBLEM 20

I N THE THREE TABLETS BELOW, THE THREE FOUR-DIGIT numbers are operated upon to produce a three-digit answer, represented by the letters shown. The process of operation is identical in each case. What is the answer to grid III?

1	4	3	2			
3	6	6	5	H	A	A
5	9	0	8			

I

2	1	3	1			
4	5	5	4	B	I	B
6	9	7	7			

II

1	0	1	7			
2	9	3	3			
4	7	6	5			

III

Solution on page 178

PROBLEM 21

A MERCHANT IS TRAVELLING FROM THINIS TO ABYDOS. Travelling is cooler than sitting still in the daylight, so he does not want to arrive until dusk, but he is tired and thirsty, so he does not want to arrive after dusk. If he sets his speed at 300 khet an hour, he will be an hour early. If he travels at 200 khet an hour, he will be an hour late. What speed should he set?

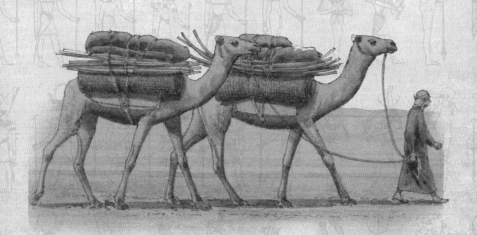

Solution on page 178

PROBLEM 22

————◆————

THERE IS AN ART TO THE CONSTRUCTION OF THE PERFECT LABYRINTH.
Clearly, there are some well-established guidelines that are worth following.
At the same time however, it is important to recognise that for true security, a less
familiar element needs to be incorporated.

This trial will provide you with the basis for a labyrinth layout that is grounded
in mathematics. The cells of the grid below each hold a number from 1 to 14. In any
given row or column, some numbers may be duplicated. Your challenge is to block
out duplicates so that no number is repeated in any single line, horizontal or vertical.
In addition to that, you need to ensure that no two blocked cells are in horizontal or
vertical contact with each other. It is also necessary to make certain that you can get
from any unblocked cell to all others, moving orthogonally, without having to cross a
blocked cell.

1	14	14	5	10	10	2	8	12	7
13	4	13	3	3	7	1	5	4	14
2	13	4	10	6	9	12	12	8	4
7	3	14	11	11	8	6	2	9	6
6	12	5	8	12	8	10	5	13	1
12	11	1	10	5	10	8	6	3	12
9	7	5	11	13	9	12	6	5	6
13	11	8	13	9	11	7	14	4	9
8	10	6	2	5	5	8	8	1	12
11	8	1	6	1	3	14	4	11	13
1	12	7	3	3	3	4	8	2	8
12	5	4	4	14	1	8	7	12	9
8	9	4	2	2	14	3	3	14	11
5	5	2	9	7	14	14	10	11	11

Solution on page 179

PROBLEM 23

T HE KEEPER OF ALE FOUND HIMSELF WITH A PROBLEM
earlier. I suspect that you would have been able to advise
him properly, Great One. He found himself with just three jars.
The largest, an 8 hinu jar, was full of ale. The two smaller jars,
measuring 5 hinu and 3 hinu, were both empty. He needed
to prepare two four-hinu measures of ale. What is the most
effective way that he could do so without resorting to guesswork
or finding some extra measuring devices?

solution on page 180

PROBLEM 24

THIS PATTERN FOLLOWS A CERTAIN MATHEMATICAL LOGIC.
How many points does the question mark represent?

Solution on page 180

PROBLEM 25

A GROUP OF FRIENDS ARE AT THE LOCAL TEMPLE, BUYING A consignment of chickens. If each person pays 9 debens of copper, they will have 11 debens too much. If each pays 6 debens, they will have 16 too little. How many friends are in the group?

Solution on page 181

PROBLEM 26

CAN YOU FIND YOUR WAY FROM THE TOP OF THIS labyrinth to the bottom?

Solution on page 181

PROBLEM 27

A WEALTHY MERCHANT DIED RECENTLY, LEAVING HIS WIFE pregnant. In his will, it states that if the wife bears him a son, the boy is to get two thirds of the holdings, and the wife the remaining third. On the other hand, if she bears a daughter, the wife should gets two thirds, and the daughter the remaining third. The gods, however, have been capricious. Three days ago, the wife gave birth to twins, one of either sex. What is your judgement as to the fair disposition of the man's goods according to his wishes?

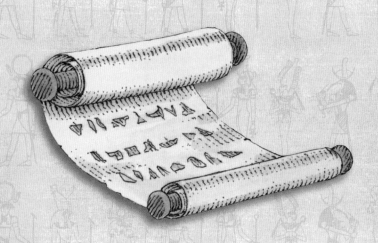

Solution on page 182

PROBLEM 28

As Anubis weighs our sins against divine Ma'at, so, mighty Pharaoh, do you weigh our lives against your Earthly law. These scales all hang true. What is the least value of whole units that each symbol may weigh?

solution on page 182

PROBLEM 29

T HE SYMBOLS IN THIS LABYRINTH APPEAR ACCORDING TO A strict order. If you uncover the underlying pattern, it will be easy to correctly complete the missing segment.

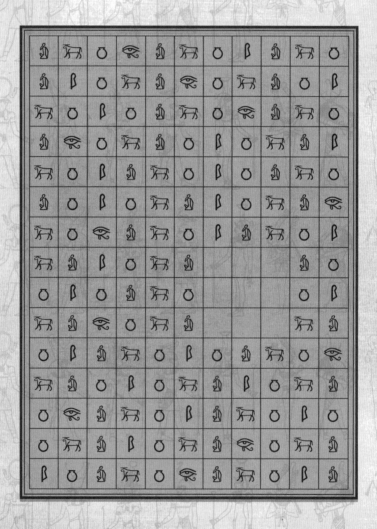

solution on page 183

PROBLEM 30

❖─◆─❖

THIS CURIOUS TABLET CAN BE DIVIDED INTO FOUR IDENTICAL shapes. Each piece thus divided contains one of each of the five symbols, as shown. What is the division?

PROBLEM 31

⟨⟨⟨ ◆ ⟩⟩⟩

Certain members of the palace guard have drawn a problem to my attention. The division of living space – a relic of the past, undoubtedly – is proving somewhat unfair. Perhaps you would favour them by sorting out a more just division of accomodation?

I have taken the liberty of preparing a representation of the living space in question for you. For each guard, I have marked down the number of months that he has been in your service. I feel that it would be sensible to allocate each man a simple rectangular space equal in squares to the duration of his service to date. Can you enclose each man in a rectangular space exactly equal to his length of service, so that no two spaces overlap, and no space is left over?

7							
	21						
					15		
			35				
					30		
			18				
		24					

⟨ Solution on page 184 ⟩

PROBLEM 32

M y Pharaoh, it may have occurred to you that we count in batches of ten. We have ten separate unique digits. When we write '10', we mean "One lot of ten, and none extra." '100' indicates one lot of ten times ten. But this is not the only way. The Babylonians, for example, count in batches of sixty, as did the Sumerians before them. It can be helpful to gain some practice with the idea of different counting systems. If one counted in batches of 5, so that "100" meant twenty-five, what would the number ninety-five look like?

Solution on page 185

PROBLEM 33

A PAIR OF LABOURERS HAVE BEEN TENDING THE TREES IN ONE
of your ornamental gardens today, mighty Pharaoh. Ahnen
and Bata were assigned one half of the garden each, the number
of trees being the same in both halves. Ahnen started first, took
the right-hand side of the garden, and began working. He had
seen to three trees when Bata arrived, and declared that Ahnen
was dealing with the wrong side. Ahnen obediently swapped
to the left side. The men then worked through the morning. As
noon approached, Bata finished his side of the garden, and then
decided to help Ahnen get his half completed. Bata cared for
six trees before the work was completed. Who tended the most
trees, and by what quantity?

solution on page 185

PROBLEM 34

A MOST PECULIAR THING OCCURRED TO ME DURING MY SLEEP LAST NIGHT. I was visited by a hairy, bearded dwarf, who identified himself as Bes. He waved his hand in front of my eyes, and showed me a glorious vision. As I awoke in startlement, the vision faded, leaving behind it a memory of numbers. I wrote them down swiftly, of course. It seems to me that the numbers contain the information required to recrea te my vision. Each one represents a group of blocks to be shaded along that horizontal or vertical line, separated from any other group by at least one space. When both horizontal and vertical are taken into account, one of your divine blood will surely be able to help me recreate the god's vision.

Row clues (top to bottom):

1.1
3.3
1.3.1
1.1.1
1.1.1
1.1.4
7.2
2.6
1.3.1.1
3.2.1.2.6
6.3.1.1
2.6
1.1.1
1.5.7
3.4.2.1
1.10
1.1.1
2.10
5.1.7
18
9.8
19
9.8
19

Column clues (left to right):

1. 2
2. 3
3. 1.1.1
4. 1.1
5. 1
6. 2.1.4
7. 1.1.5
8. 1.1.6
9. 1.1.6
10. 1.1.2.7
11. 1.1.1.5
12. 6.3.1.1.5
13. 6.3.1.5
14. 2.1.1.5.1.1
15. 2.1.2.1.1.1
16. 5.1.2.1.5
17. 2.2.1.1.7
18. 2.1.1.7.7
19. 5.1.1.1.1.7
20. 1.1.1.1.7
21. 3.1.1.1.1.7
22. 4.1.1.1.7
23. 15

Solution on page 186

PROBLEM 35

I N THIS CUNNING LABYRINTH OF NUMBERS, YOU ARE REQUIRED TO move cautiously, horizontally or vertically, always stepping from 2 to 4 to 6, then 8, 0, and back to 2 again. Starting from a 2 on the top row, your task is to find a route to the bottom — and the sum of all of its steps, added together, must total 280.

2	4	2	4	8	2	6	2	4	2	0	2
2	6	8	6	4	2	0	8	6	4	6	4
6	2	4	8	2	4	6	4	8	8	4	0
6	4	2	0	6	2	2	6	4	4	8	2
8	2	4	2	8	8	4	2	2	2	0	8
0	2	6	4	6	6	8	6	8	0	2	6
2	6	0	6	4	0	2	8	6	6	4	4
4	6	8	0	2	4	0	8	4	2	6	8
2	6	6	8	6	6	8	0	2	0	2	0
4	4	2	6	8	6	6	0	6	6	4	2
6	2	4	2	4	4	4	2	0	8	6	0
8	8	6	4	0	8	6	6	2	4	6	2
0	4	2	8	2	8	2	4	0	2	4	8
4	6	8	6	4	2	4	8	8	6	8	6
6	2	0	6	2	0	2	2	4	2	0	4
2	0	2	4	6	2	8	0	2	4	6	0
8	4	4	6	8	0	6	4	6	0	8	2
2	8	6	8	0	2	4	0	2	8	0	8
6	0	6	0	6	4	8	8	6	4	2	6
4	2	4	6	2	6	4	0	4	2	8	4

solution on page 187

PROBLEM 36

I T CAN BE DISTRACTING TO COMPARE OBJECTS WHICH ARE mirrored into different orientations. Even the most familiar of likenesses — such as this one of Amun, your heavenly father — can become somewhat confusing. There are four reflections of the Self-Created shown here; only one is the exact match to the larger image. Which is it?

Solution on page 188

PROBLEM 37

A S THE SCRIBE WOULD SAY — POSSIBLY TALKING ABOUT A small volume of sand — one amount plus its quarter is 16. What is the amount?

solution on page 188

PROBLEM 38

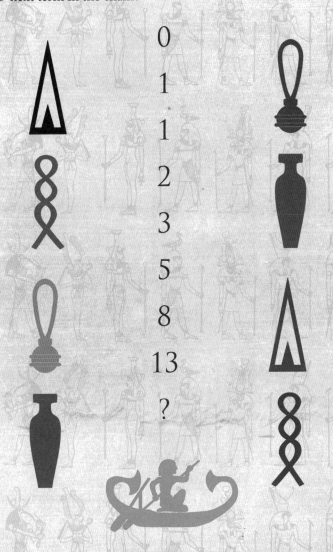

These numbers follow a strict sequence. What is the next term in the chain?

0
1
1
2
3
5
8
13
?

Solution on page 189

PROBLEM 39

———◆———

T HE MATTER OF FAIRNESS IN DEALING IS OFTEN CRITICAL.
Yesterday, in the evening, our chief cook purchased wheat
from one of the many merchants. He bought 12 hekats, of
assorted qualities. Two hekats were of lesser-grade wheat, and
were thus 40% cheaper than the regular grain. One hekat was
low-grade, and 75% cheaper. On the other hand, two hekats
were of high-grade grain, 25% more expensive than usual. The
total cost was 219 deben of copper. How much is a single hekat
of standard-grade wheat?

Solution on page 189

PROBLEM 40

THERE IS A GAME THAT IS PLAYED IN THE REACHES OF lower Egypt with small, polished cubes of bone or hard wood. The faces of each cube are numbered from 1 to 6, and they are cast to yield a number at random. Some wagering takes place on nothing so complex as the amount of sixes obtained. Do you think it is easier to roll six cubes and get at least one '6', to roll twelve cubes and get at least two '6's, or to roll eighteen cubes and get at least three '6's?

Solution on page 190

PROBLEM 41

Form defines substance. The shapes taken by the Gods encapsulate their very essence. They could not be other than they are, no more than you yourself could be other. Set, the ruler of the desert, is shown here. Four pitch-black likenesses stand beside him, but only one of them is truly the Lord of Storm. Which is it?

Solution on page 190

PROBLEM 42

HE WHO PACIFIES THE TWO LANDS, IT CAN BE SURPRISING how swiftly a situation can multiply to engulf all. For the sake of illustration, imagine that rabbits breed just once in every month, and give birth to just one rabbit of each sex. These young pairs mature over their first month, and then breed from the second month after their birth. How many rabbits will there be after twelve months, if all goes well for them?

solution on page 190

PROBLEM 43

A TABLET HAS BEEN BROKEN INTO MANY PIECES. THE ILLUSTRATION SHOWS HOW the tablet looked, as well as the pieces that it has fallen into. Can you see how to reassemble it?

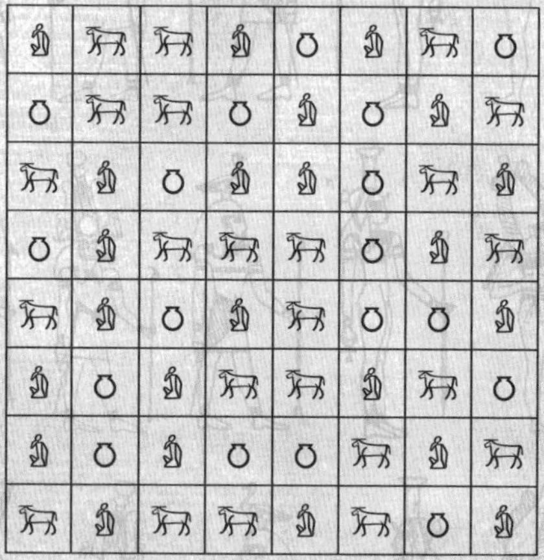

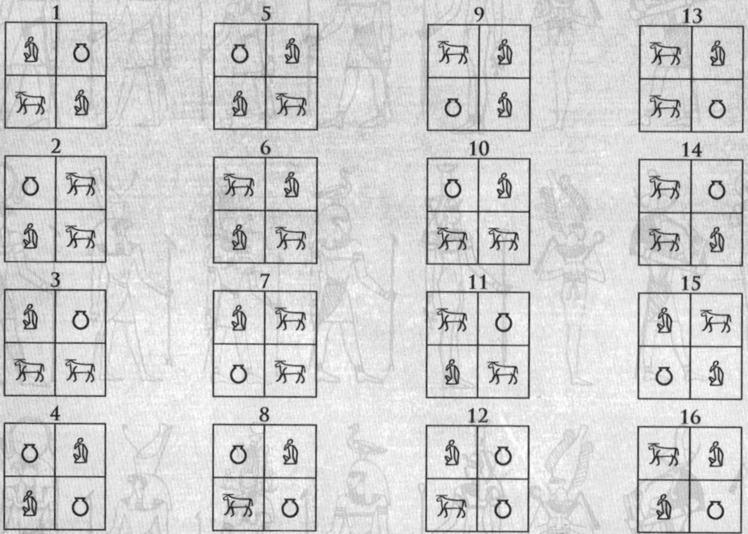

solution on page 190

PROBLEM 44

I T IS WELL KNOWN THAT BRAVE MEHEN, THE COILED ONE, LOOPS HIMSELF AROUND Ra each night as the Sun journeys through the darkness of the underworld, helping to keep Apep the slitherer at bay. These voyages can be complex, far more so than the relatively simple course the Morning Boat steers through our skies during than the day. Priests of the Sun have scried the course of such a journey, but their minds lack the divinity required to untangle Mehen's precise movements. It is known that he forms himself into a single gigantic loop, tail caught by mouth, inside which Ra can benefit from his protective efforts.

In this representation, they have prepared a square grid, the lines of which represent spaced which Mehen's body might occupy. Many cells of the grid contain a number which the Priests have certified as representing the number of sides of that cell that Mehen's mighty body lies against. So a cell with the number 3 in has all but one side closed off by his length; a cell holding 0 is untouched, save perhaps at the very instant of a corner. For some cells, the priests remain sadly uncertain.

It would be most helpful to the poor priests if you would lend yourself to plotting the exact pattern formed by Mehen's body.

2	1		2		2	3				
	2		1	3				2		2
2	2	0		2		1		2		1	2
	2	3	2			3	1		2	
1		2	2		3	2		1	2	2
2		3		2	2		3	2		3
	2	2	2		1		0		2	2
1		1	1		3		2			3
3		3	3	1		1	2	3		3
	1			2	3	1	2	1	1	2
3									2	
	1	3		3				2		

Solution on page 191

PROBLEM 45

S HOWN HERE ARE TWO IMAGES OF NUIT, MISTRESS OF ALL,
ruler of the skies. Some imperfections have crept into the
second image, perhaps because of Tenenet's ever-seductive
influence. There are nine errors in total. Can you find them?

solution on page 192

PROBLEM 46

O UR SCOUTS HAVE GATHERED INTELLIGENCE REGARDING a potentially hostile encampment on the borders of Punt. From outside the perimeter of the encampment, they have been able to ascertain the number of troop tents in any given slice of the groups. They have not been able to give absolutely precise locations, but they have confirmed that each tent is connected to an orthogonally adjacent tree. Every tree is occupied.

It would be of undoubted assistance to know the specific location of each tent. I am confident that your prowess will enable you to identify the precise positions with ease.

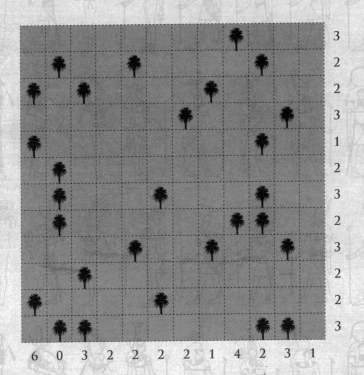

solution on page 193

PROBLEM 47

THIS GRID IS MADE UP OF A NUMBER OF PAIRS OF TOKENS. Each individual token represents a number, and the totals at the end of each row and column are the value of the sum of each of number in that line. What value does each token hold?

				30
				39
				28
21	25	26	25	

Solution on page 194

PROBLEM 48

THIS GRID REPRESENTS A PROBLEM OF CHAMBERS. I AM HAPPY TO NOTE THAT THE situation is hypothetical, rather than literal, but solving it will undoubtedly prove useful when it comes to preparing for that blessed day when you resume your place amongst the Gods.

In the diagram, you can see a range of numbers placed into a simple grid. Each number is part of a chamber. The chamber contains exactly as many floor tiles as the number on those tiles. So a floor tile containing a '1' is a self-contained single-square chamber, whilst a tile containing a '4' is connected to three other tiles like itself. Most of the numbers are hidden, but the grid is completely used. All the tiles in one chamber are connected by touching, and no chamber directly touches another chamber of the same size at any point. Diagonal connections are not considered to be touching. Your goal is to calculate the extent of each chamber.

Solution on page 194

PROBLEM 49

THREE TYPES OF SOULS STOOD IN A PACK BEFORE ANUBIS, for the weighing of the heart. As you would expect, virtuous souls were confident in their rectitude and always told the truth, whilst damned souls, consumed by their own iniquity, could do naught but lie. Those whose fate remained uncertain were less predictable, and could speak either truth or falsehood as they saw fit. In this pack, there were 90 souls, divided into three groups. It is known that one group of 30 was made up entirely of one type of soul, another was split exactly into halves between two of the three types, and the final group comprised an even mix of all three types, ten of each. In no particular order, one of these groups of 30 declared themselves all virtuous. A second all bemoaned their damnation. The final group announced that all its members were unsure of what would come. How many souls were truly of uncertain fate?

⚮ solution on page 195 ⚮

PROBLEM 50

◆————◆◆————◆

For this problem, the number in the courtyard is obtained through performing mathematical operations on the numbers in the towers surrounding it. The same process is applied to each courtyard. What number should be in the final courtyard?

8   4   3   9

[14]   [13]

7   9   4   5

7   2   6   1

[12]   [?]

3   6   3   4

Solution on page 195

MEDIUM PUZZLES

Lord of All, Nebkheperure, Pleaser of the Gods, it falls to me to here note that this is the point where the more straightforward problems give way to those of middling difficulty. I have no doubt that both will seem equally trivial to your divine intellect, but should you choose to show this scroll to simple mortals, I hope that they will consider this warning of some use.

PROBLEM 51

If these tiles

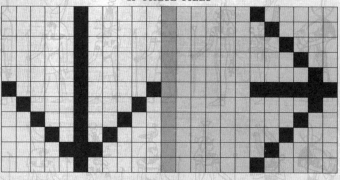

yield this result:

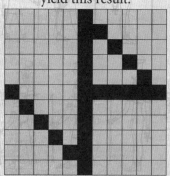

Then what do these tiles yield?

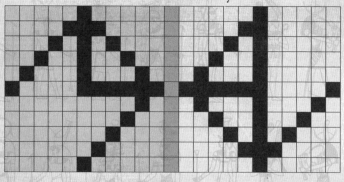

Solution on page 197

PROBLEM 52

P LEASER OF THE GODS, CONSIDER THIS ARRANGEMENT OF beams, rods and weights. It is in exact balance. The beams and rods have been cunningly made so as to be perfectly stiff, and to counterweight each other exactly around the pivot, so that their weights may be discounted entirely. How much does the block with the question mark weigh?

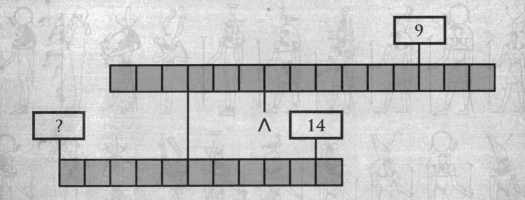

Solution on page 198

PROBLEM 53

T HERE IS NO MATTER AS SERIOUS AS THE WEIGHT OF innocence versus justice. These scales all hang in perfect balance, as do the hearts of those true enough to join the ranks of the living. What is the least number of whole units that each symbol may weigh?

solution on page 198

PROBLEM 54

THIS IS ANOTHER CONSIGNMENT OF COUNTERFEIT ICONS, this time of mighty Ra himself, the Caller of Life. The priests of the Lord of Truth are significantly unamused. Six of the icons are fake, and bear errors. Which pair are the originals?

Solution on page 199

PROBLEM 55

THIS TABLET CONTAIN LONG-FORGOTTEN MYSTIC WISDOM. It can be divided into four identical shapes, each containing the eight symbols shown below. What is the division?

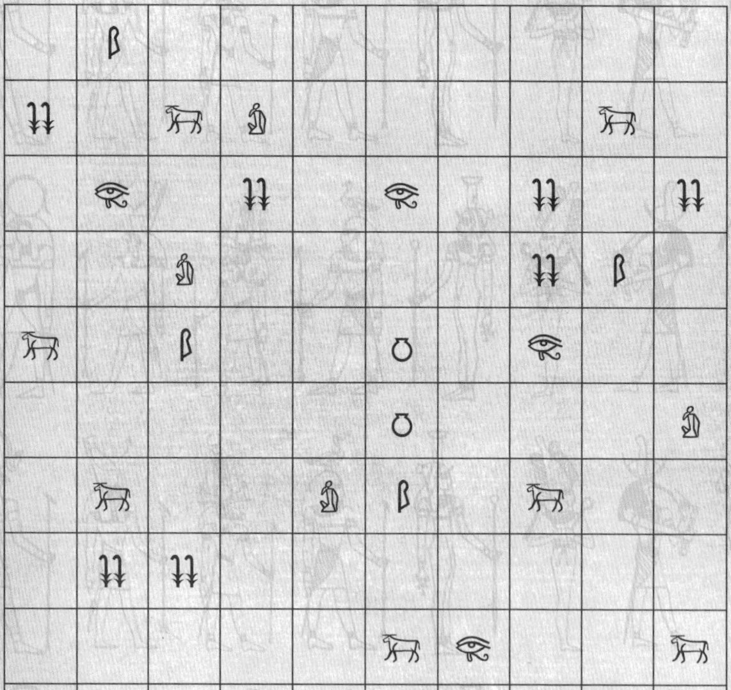

Solution on page 199

PROBLEM 56

E ACH NUMBER REPRESENTS AN ARCHER STATIONED IN THE FIELD. There are obstructions to his line of fire, which are not shown but occupy a single square each. Each archer reports the number of squares in the field that he can see, vertically or horizontally, including the square he is on. So a man reporting four squares is able to see his own space and just three others. Archers do not obstruct each other, and do not stand on obstructions. No two obstructions are in horizontal or vertical contact. Can you calculate the precise extent of each man's range?

				7					6	
11		9					9			
			4			5				
		13		13						
7	9		9							
						8				
			6							
							6		9	9
					6		2			
			7			2				
		9						8		7
	13				7					

꙰ solution on page 200 ꙰

PROBLEM 57

I N A NEARBY MARKET YESTERDAY, I HAPPENED TO OVERHEAR three men discussing the possible purchase of an exotic beast, priced at 24 debens. None of the men had quite enough to buy the animal outright. The first one said, "If I borrow half of the money you two have between you, I'll have enough." The second one said, "Well, if I borrowed two thirds of what you two have, I'd have enough with half a deben left over." The third one said, "If I borrowed three quarters of the money you two are carrying, I'd be able to buy it with one and a half debens remaining." How much does each man have?

Solution on page 200

PROBLEM 58

THE JUST DISTRIBUTION OF REWARDS CAN QUICKLY BECOME a matter of some complexity. Consider the matter of shares. There are 10 people who are to share 10 hekats of grain, but not evenly. The first person receives the largest share; each subsequent person gets 1/8th of a hekat less than the person immediately before. If there is to be no grain left over, then what is the largest share?

Solution on page 201

PROBLEM 59

A SNAIL ACCIDENTALLY FALLS INTO AN EARTHY PIT THAT IS four and a half cubits deep. Trying to get out, it climbs up two cubits on its first day, but slips back down 1 cubit during the night. The process is tiring, and every subsequent day it climbs, it manages to go only 90% as far as the day before. It still slips the same distance during the night, however. When will it escape (or be forced to accept its new home)?

solution on page 202

PROBLEM 60

T HESE GRIDS FORM A SEQUENCE, A PROGRESSION AS UNTO THE march of time itself. What should the fourth grid look like?

1

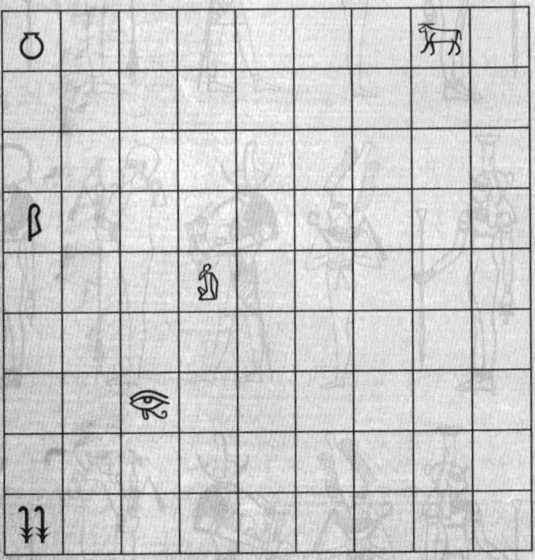

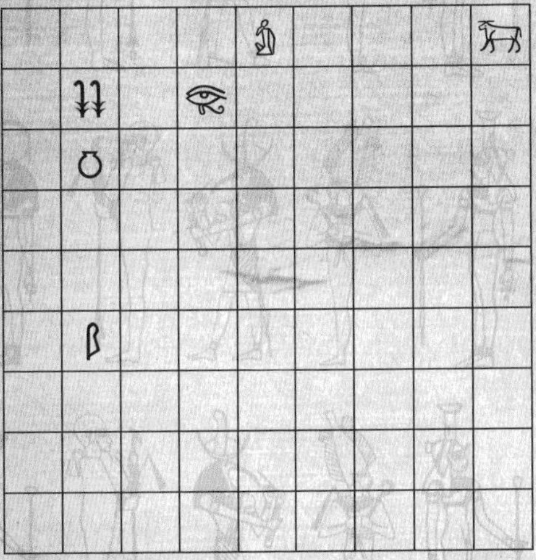

3

2

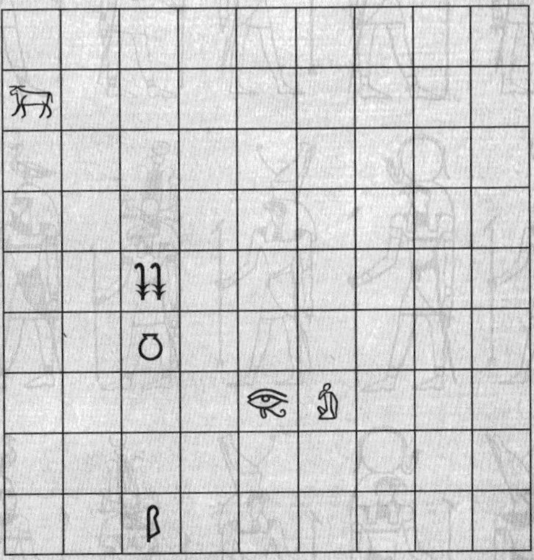

4

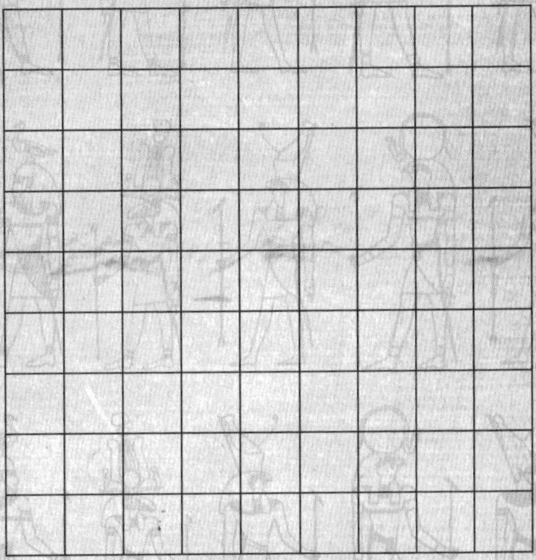

Solution on page 202

PROBLEM 61

W HAT IS THE ROUTE YOU NEED TO TAKE TO GET FROM THE
entrance of this labyrinth to its exit?

Solution on page 203

PROBLEM 62

THREE SONS INHERIT 30 PRECIOUS JARS FROM THEIR FATHER, to be divided evenly. Ten of the jars are full of valuable unguents. Ten more are half-full. The remaining ten are empty. How can the jars be distributed so that each son gets his full share of ten containers and five full measures of unguent, and also receives at least one of each type of jar?

Solution on page 204

PROBLEM 63

I AM INFORMED THAT THE SARDESIAN DOCK MANAGERS HELP to while away the time by contriving increasingly tricky grids for the workers to pile crates onto. To recap, each square of the grid holds a pile of between 1 and 7 crates. Each row and column holds exactly one of each size of pile, and some piles are specified as being larger than others. Completing the grid pattern from the arrangement shown here should offer you a certain amount of diversion.

Solution on page 205

PROBLEM 64

C ONSIDER THESE GAME BOARDS, WHICH I AM TOLD come from Naqaba.

If

is worth 29 and

is worth 82,
then how much is

worth?

Solution on page 206

PROBLEM 65

❦——◆——❦

Turn your mind, if you will, to a large heap of sand. If you take one grain away, it is still a heap. Keep taking grains away, one by one, and the heap will slowly shrink, but it remains undeniably still a heap. How about when there is just one grain left? Is it still a heap? If not, when did it stop being a heap? Something is clearly wrong, but what?

⚖ solution on page 206 ⚖

PROBLEM 66

Dread Sobek, the ferocious creator, is shown here in his power and glory. His likeness has been mirrored four times. Only one of the four is a perfect reflection of Nile's fearsome protector, however. Which is it?

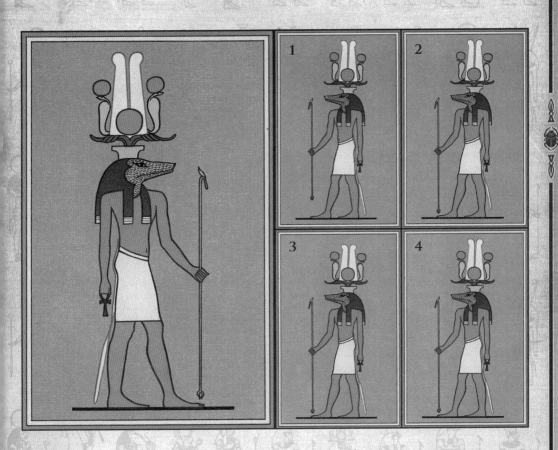

Solution on page 207

PROBLEM 67

A QUANTITY OF DATES, TOGETHER WITH 2/3 OF ITSELF, has a third of its total number taken away to yield 10. What is the quantity?

Solution on page 207

PROBLEM 68

⬥

THIS MAGICAL SQUARE OF NUMBERS IS SO CUNNINGLY devised that its every row and column add up to the same total, as do its two major diagonals. The sets of three numbers each fit into one of the empty horizontal groups on the grid. But where do they go?

			41			
			17			
			49			
13	31	7	25	43	19	37
			1			
			33			
			9			

18, 36, 12	21, 39, 8
46, 15, 40	22, 47, 16
2, 27, 45	42, 11, 29
30, 6, 24	26, 44, 20
38, 14, 32	34, 3, 28
10, 35, 4	5, 23, 48

Solution on page 208

PROBLEM 69

A MECHANICAL TIME-MEASURING DEVICE TAKES THE FORM of a circle, with sweeping bars that move at different rate. The shortest bar makes a complete rotation two times a day, measuring 12 hours of light and 12 of darkness. The middle bar makes a complete rotation once each standard hour, as is considered to indicate sixty divisions of a minute. The longest bar, which moves fastest, makes a complete rotation sixty times an hour, once every minute. At exactly 8 o'clock, the short bar will be two thirds of the way around the face, whilst the other two will be precisely vertical. To the nearest second, what will be the time when the three bars next align together?

solution on page 208

PROBLEM 70

T HE HEAVENLY REED FIELDS ARE A BEAUTIFUL PARADISE OF peace and contentment. Those virtuous enough to dwell amongst them take their leisure amongst the islands. Naturally, in any dominion, it is possible to move from any one island to any other, though the route may not always be direct. The paths of Aaru are straight, never deviating nor crossing one another, although some are singular, and some are parallel double-paths. In this illustrated dominion, the islands alone are shown, and each island proudly displays the number of paths that touches it. How do the islands connect?

2			6		3		
				1		2	
3		2		1			
	2			3	5		
3	5		7		4		
1	1						
			4	3			
2							
1		2	2				
5	7	6	4				
1							
2		1	3				
2	4	3	3				

Solution on page 209

PROBLEM 71

I N THE THREE TABLETS BELOW, THE THREE FOUR-DIGIT
numbers are operated upon to produce a three-digit answer,
represented by the letters shown. The process of operation is
identical in each case. What is the answer to grid III?

I

1	7	6	6			
2	1	4	5	E	B	F
4	0	0	0			

II

0	9	1	7			
1	8	1	6	C	G	D
5	0	0	0			

III

4	9	3	9			
2	7	4	1			
6	0	0	0			

solution on page 210

PROBLEM 72

❖

Consider this, mighty one. Bes, standing on a table, drops a ball from 1.44m above the floor. Each bounce, it regains precisely three quarters of the maximum height that it knew previously. It will stop when its maximum height is less than 1cm from the ground. How many bounces will this take?

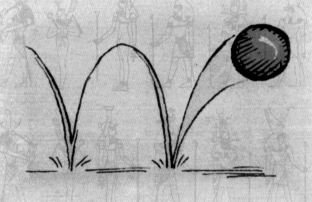

ᕰ Solution on page 210 ᕰ

PROBLEM 73

HERE ARE TWO SETS OF MATHEMATICAL OPERATIONS, WITH their answers. The digits have been replaced by symbols, which are consistent in both sets. What is the missing number?

×

=   99   ⌇⌇⌇   ß   ⌇⌇⌇   +

=   2   5   3   2   8

99   ×

?   ?

=   ß   +

=   3   5   4   0   1

Solution on page 211

PROBLEM 74

THIS MYCENEAN GRID IS SOMEWHAT MORE CHALLENGING than the former, but no less entertaining or salutory. As before, paired tiles have to be connected by a single, unbroken line of tiles, connected horizontally or vertically without any redundant loops. No two lines cross. Two indicated tiles play no part, but the rest of the grid is filled. Can you find the paths?

Solution on page 211

PROBLEM 75

T HIS PROBLEM LINKS THREE PAIRS OF NUMBERS TO A
common answer, through varied mathematical operations.
What is the central number?

Solution on page 212

PROBLEM 76

T HE DARK SQUARES ON THESE FOUR BOARDS NEED TO BE combined into a summary board. They do not combine simply, however. If a square is dark on just one board, or on all four boards, then it is dark on the summary board. Otherwise, it remains unshaded. What does the summary board look like?

Solution on page 212

PROBLEM 77

⸺ ◆ ⸺

MIGHTY RULER OF TRUTH, THE EQUATIONS SHOWN HERE are accurate, save that the whole numbers involved in the operations have been replaced. Calculations are performed strictly in the order they appear on each line, so what are the numbers?

$$\text{[man]} + \text{[ox]} - \text{[duck]} + \text{[plants]} = 12$$

$$\text{[plants]} + \text{[duck]} - \text{[man]} - \text{[ox]} = 10$$

$$\text{[duck]} \times \text{[ox]} + \text{[plants]} - \text{[man]} = 43$$

$$\text{[ox]} - \text{[man]} \times \text{[plants]} - \text{[duck]} = 15$$

$$\text{[plants]} - \text{[ox]} / \text{[man]} \times \text{[duck]} = 14$$

Solution on page 212

PROBLEM 78

T HE PALACE GUARDSMEN THAT YOU GENEROUSLY ACCOMMODATED RECENTLY HAVE been greatly pleased with their new room allocations. They have been praising your wisdom far and wide. Accordingly, a second group, somewhat larger than the first, have also petitioned for similar treatment. It would be a generous gesture to so favour them. As before, I have made a note of the available space, and the number of months than each guard has been in service. I would appreciate it if you could take an instant or two to divide the space up so that each man is enclosed by a simple rectangular room, equal in squares to the length of his service. No rooms should overlap, nor should there be any space unallocated.

Solution on page 213

PROBLEM 79

T HERE ARE LIMITLESS WAYS, POTENTIALLY, OF ORGANISING how numbers are written. We write our numbers in base ten, where our numbers mean single units, batches of ten, batches of ten times ten, and so on. If the number 10240 is written in base 6, where 100 means 'thirty-six', how much does it represent in base ten?

Solution on page 214

PROBLEM 80

❖

I MAGINE THAT THREE ORNATE BUT IDENTICAL BOXES ARE placed before you. Each holds two one-kite pieces. In one box, both kites are gold. In a second, they are both silver. In the third, there is one of each. You close your eyes, and pick one kite from one box, and then open them to discover that it is gold. What is the likelihood that the other kite in the box is also gold?

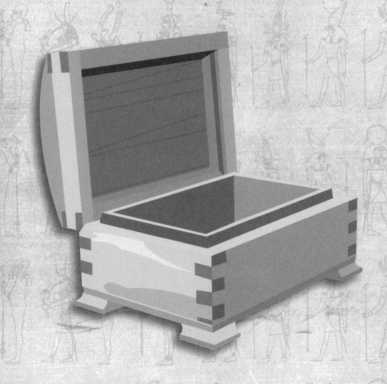

Solution on page 214

PROBLEM 81

W HEN THE FALCON FLIES BEFORE THE SUN, IT MAY BE
recognised only by its shape. In this way, mighty Horus,
the One Above, is sometimes shrouded in darkness. This
likeness here shows him at rest. Beside him is his silhouette,
along with three deceptive shadows that are not quite correct.
Which is true?

solution on page 214

PROBLEM 82

T HE SCALES OF JUSTICE ARE INTIMATELY FAMILIAR TO ALL merchants, who are well versed in finding the correct weights and balances. There is benefit, of course, in carrying as small a selection of measuring weights as possible. What is the least number of measuring weights required to balance a load of up to 121 deben, and how much does each one weigh?

Solution on page 214

PROBLEM 83

——◆——

THIS IMAGE DEPICTS A NOW-BROKEN TABLET. ITS VARIOUS COMPONENT
pieces are also shown. Can you see how to reassemble it?

PROBLEM 84

⸺◆⸺

THE PRIESTS OF RA HAVE RETURNED WITH ANOTHER SET of divinations regarding the disposition of coiled Mehen during his nightly duties. They apologise that this is somewhat less certain than the last.

As before, Mehen's snaking body lies along some of the dotted lines in the grid below, forming one single gigantic loop. In each cell that they are certain of, the priests have recorded the number of sides of that cell which Mehen's body occupies. If you would extend your forbearance, they would be most grateful for your analysis of precisely where Mehen lies.

```
 2  3  .  3  .  3  .  .  3  3
 .  2  .  .  .  0  2  .  .  .
 .  .  .  .  .  3  .  .  2  3
 3  2  .  .  2  0  .  .  .  3
 .  3  .  .  .  2  .  3  .  2  2
 3  3  .  1  .  2  2  .  2  .  2
 .  1  .  .  3  .  .  0  .  .
 2  1  .  .  .  2  .  3  .  .
 .  1  .  .  .  2  .  .  1  .  2  2
 .  .  .  2  2  2  .  1  .  3
 2  .  1  1  0  2  .  2  .  .  1
 2  .  .  2  .  .  3  .  .  3
```

⸎ Solution on page 215 ⸎

PROBLEM 85

A MAN IS TRAINING HIS HOUND. HE TAKES THE BEAST A whole iteru from their home, and unleashes it. It proceeds to run home, and then immediately turns around and runs back towards the man. When it gets back to him, it immediately heads back for home again, and so on, running back and forth. At the same time, the man starts walking back towards home at a comfortable pace. The dog continues running until the man reaches the house. The creature is capable of running an iteru in one hour, and keeping that pace up for several hours at a stretch. The man on the other hand, walks just two fifths of an iteru in one hour. How far will the hound run, from the moment of its release to the man's return to his house?

Solution on page 216

PROBLEM 86

Bes has visited me with another of his visions. I truly feel blessed. As before, the image faded into numbers as I awoke, and I duly recorded them. Each separate number represents a group of shaded blocks in that horizontal or vertical line. Groups are continuous, and separated from each other by at least one empty block. By cross-referencing them, you will be able to reveal this mystery.

3
1.1
1.1.2
3.1.2
2.1.3.2
2.1.1.3
2.3
3.3
3.5
2.3
3.6.5
1.1.5.3.1
3.1.2.2.1.3.1
1.1.1.1.4.1.1.1
1.1.1.2.5.2.1.1
1.1.1.1.5.1.2
1.1.1.3.5.1.1
1.1.1.1.3.2
1.1.1.4.1
1.1.1.1.2
1.1.1.6.2
1.1.1.3
1.1.1.3.3.1
1.1.1.5.4

13	1	1	2	2	2	1	3	1	1	1	1	1	3	1	2	1	2	2	2	1	1	1	7
		14	1	15	2	1	2	1	2	1	2	1	2	1	1	1	2	1	2	1	2	1	
						1	9	1	1	2	3	1	1	1	8	1	1	3	1	1			
							1	2	1	1	1	7	5	5	1	3	2	3	4				
								1	1	1	1	1	1	2		4	1	1	1				
								1	1	1		2											
								1	1														
								1															
								2															

Solution on page 216

PROBLEM 87

In this maze of numbers, you are required to start somewhere on the top row, and finish by reaching the bottom row. You may move horizontally or vertically without restriction, totalling the value of the squares you step on as you go. However, stepping on or next to a zero wipes your score thus far. This is true even if you just pass diagonally adjacent to a 0, such is its power. Your task is to find a route totalling 170 points.

3	5	6	4	1	5		6	8	4	2	3
5	2	4	8	6	7			5	3	6	2
7	8	9	9	2	3	4		1	8	1	4
9	7	2	2	4	8	2		0	7	3	7
2	9	7	6	5	9				3	5	5
1	6	5	3	2	8				9	2	3
3	2	1	5	1	6	5			1	7	5
0	8	6	1	9	2	3			2	5	9
8	6	3	7	7	4	5		9	3	4	7
	2	7	8	3	3	7	3	5	6	1	8
		8	1	0	8	4	3	6	4		
6			6	5	3	7	2	5			
3	7	8		1	6	2	1				
3	4	8	4		9	0	4	3			
6	3	3		3	5	6	2				
2	3	5		2	4	8	6	7	3		
1	7	7		9	2	3	6	5	1		
6	0	3	5	7	6	4	1	8	9		
8	2	1	4	2	8	4	7	4	2	5	
9	3	5	7	3	8	2	1	2	7	4	3

Solution on page 217

PROBLEM 88

THREE PRIESTS ARE EACH ESCORTING A NOVICE PRIESTESS TO a temple at Karnak. They meet whilst seeking to cross the Great River near Naqada. The coracle that is available to them to cross with can hold just two people, and it would dismay any of the young novices to be in the presence of an unfamiliar man without her guardian also being present. What is the most efficient way for the three pairs to cross, remembering that the boat cannot get back across the river on its own?

Solution on page 218

PROBLEM 89

A TWISTING LABYRINTH IS WAITING TO BE UNVEILED IN THIS test. In each horizontal or vertical line of this grid, you have to ensure that no number appears twice. Duplicates are to be blocked out. There are some restrictions, however. Squares are held to be in contact with each other either horizontally or vertically. No two blocked squares may be in contact, but every unblocked square has to remain in indirect contact with every other. When you have completed the pattern, there must be just one sprawling group of unblocked cells, with no number duplicated in any line.

6	7	1	8	5	5	7	8	11	11
9	4	7	10	3	8	1	14	10	5
1	3	4	2	2	14	9	8	9	4
3	3	8	4	4	7	10	2	5	14
12	12	7	4	8	9	9	4	7	8
11	5	6	1	5	2	14	9	13	8
2	1	2	1	13	12	12	6	4	4
12	13	2	6	2	7	5	7	14	13
10	9	12	2	14	5	2	9	4	13
5	7	13	5	7	10	12	3	13	2
5	8	9	9	12	2	11	6	2	6
8	9	5	10	9	11	5	4	11	7
2	6	9	6	7	12	4	13	12	11
13	8	3	7	13	9	8	3	1	7

Solution on page 219

PROBLEM 90

Two fathers and two sons are fishing in the Nile, they catch exactly three fish between them, but when they head home each of them has a fish. How can this be?

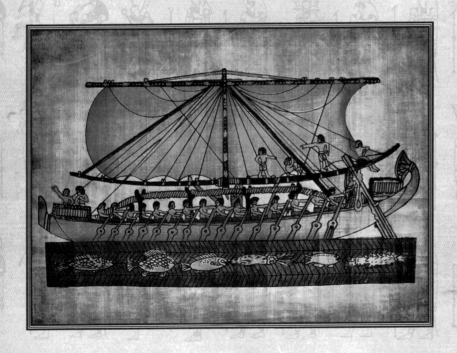

Solution on page 219

PROBLEM 91

T HIS PATTERN FOLLOWS A CERTAIN MATHEMATICAL LOGIC.
How many points does the question mark represent?

PROBLEM 92

T HE APPEARANCE OF SYMBOLS IN THIS GRID FOLLOWS A strict order. The challenge here is to complete the missing segment by correctly identifying the pattern.

Solution on page 220

PROBLEM 93

C ONSIDER THIS CHAIN OF NUMBERS. THEY FOLLOW a specific sequence. What comes next?

2 4 6 30 32 34 ?

solution on page 220

PROBLEM 94

A FULL CART OF BREAD CARRIES FIFTY LOAVES, BUT ONE
particular slave is distributing less than that. If he gives
nine men as many loaves as he can whilst making sure all have
the same number of loaves, he has two left over. If he distributes
the loaves likewise amongst four men, he is left with three. If his
distributes them amongst seven men, there are five left. How
many loaves are in the cart?

solution on page 221

PROBLEM 95

I
N THIS IMAGE, THOTH THE SCRIBE RECORDS HIS SECRETS, watched hungrily by Ammit the devourer. Our reflections of the Duat are ever imperfect, and ten discrepancies have arisen between the two renderings. Where are they?

solution on page 221

PROBLEM 96

---◆---

ANOTHER TENT CAMP HAS BEEN CAUSING YOUR GENERALS some small concern. As before, scouts have been able to examine the area from outside, and identify how many tents are to be found in each horizontal and vertical section. The trees are easier to locate precisely, but it is known that each tent is linked horizontally or vertically to one tree, although it may also abut others. Are you able to pinpoint the locations of each tent?

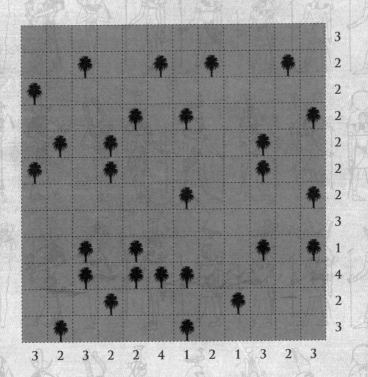

Solution on page 222

PROBLEM 97

—◆—

THERE ARE SEVERAL PAIRS OF SYMBOLS IN THIS GRID. Each symbol has a numeric value. The numbers are the end of each row and column give the total found by adding all the individual numbers in that line. What value does each symbol have?

𓃿𓃾	𓏲𓂀	𓂀𓃾	𓂀𓃒	38
𓂀𓏲	𓃾𓃒	𓃿𓏲	𓂀𓃰	33
𓃾𓃰	𓃿𓂀	𓂀𓃰	𓂀𓃾	41
31	29	26	26	

Solution on page 222

PROBLEM 98

❧◆❧

THIS IS A SLIGHTLY TRICKIER PROBLEM OF CHAMBERS. As before, the grid represents a space divided into chambers of assorted shapes and sizes. Each chamber contains one or more tiles of floor, connected from one to another either horizontally or vertically. The number on the tile tells you how many floor tiles that particular chamber encompasses. So, in an 8-tile chamber, each tile boasts the number '8'. However, most of the numbers have been obscured. Given that all the space is taken up, and that no chamber touches another of the same size horizontally or vertically, where are the chamber boundaries?

2	1					7			
				9		7			1
1			1	6	6		1	3	1
			6						3
3		1	7	7		1	6	1	4	4
9					7		1		
1						1			6
	1	2	1	3			1		8	1
	3	2							1	2
6				4		6		3		
1			1		1			3		

Solution on page 223

PROBLEM 99

Y OUR DISCERNING EAR FOR TRUTH WILL SURELY UNRAVEL
this issue swiftly, my Pharaoh. Three archers have been tested
against each other, getting four shots at a target. Three points were
awarded for a direct hit, two points for a near miss, and 1 point for
a moderate miss. I am pleased to say that every archer managed at
least a near miss. One managed four perfect shots, one managed
two hits and two near misses, and one managed one hit and
three near misses. However, they seem slightly confused as to the
results. I have three statements from each archer, and for each of
them, one of the statements is incorrect. Who scored what?

Ahmes:
    "I scored 9."
    "I scored 2 less than Baenre."
    "I scored 1 more than Djedhor."

Baenre:
    "I did not score the lowest."
    "The difference in scores between myself & Djedhor is 3."
    "Djedhor scored 12."

Djedhor:
    "I scored less than Ahmes."
    "Ahmes scored 10."
    "Baenre scored 3 more than Ahmes."

Solution on page 223

PROBLEM 100

THE CHALLENGE IN THIS PUZZLE IS TO FIND THE NUMBER missing from the final courtyard. It is deduced by performing a set of calculations upon the four surrounding towers. Each courtyard works in the same manner. What is the number?

14   11   17   9

    76   **65**

13   6   4   22

18   16   20   14

    93   **?**

13   15   12   9

Solution on page 223

HARD
PUZZLES

Beloved Lord of All, the puzzles that follow are among the most treacherous I have found. Lesser mortals would quail if their puny minds confronted such fearsome conundrums. But I am certain they will not give you even the slightest pause.

PROBLEM 101

IMAGINE FOR A MOMENT THAT YOU ARE PRESENTED WITH your choice of two identical boxes. You select one, and you are then informed that both contain a gem, but one is worth twice as much as the other. You may switch your selection. Thinking about it logically, it is clear that you should swap, because if you go from low to high you get 100% as much again, but if you go from high to low, you only lose 50%. Your potential percentage gain is twice as much as your potential loss. You may then swap again, and everything that I said before remains true. How, then, are you ever to make a decision rather than to keep swapping the boxes?

solution on page 225

PROBLEM 102

If these tiles

combine to form this one:

Then what do these tiles combine to form?

Solution on page 225

PROBLEM 103

T HE CREATOR OF THIS COMPLEX ARRANGEMENT OF BEAMS,
rods and weights is surely blessed by Ma'at, for it hangs in
exact balance. It is all of perfect stiffness, moving as one piece.
The beams and rods have been constructed with perfection so as
to counter-weight each other around the pivot. Only the values
of the weights shown thus needs to be considered. How much
does the block bearing the question mark weigh?

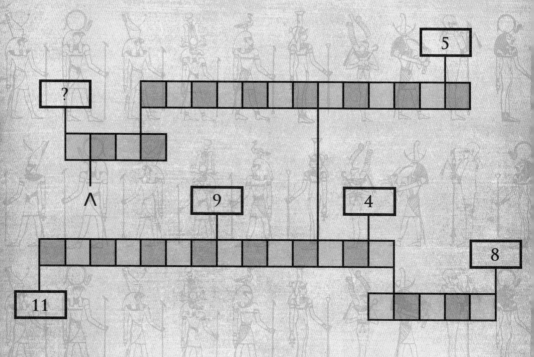

solution on page 226

PROBLEM 104

A FARMER IS TRYING TO CAPTURE A GOAT THAT HAS ESCAPED from its enclosure. The goat has a 10-cubit head start, and in its panic, it is running as hard as it can. It starts out at a speed of 10 cubits a second, but it drops its speed by one at the end of every three seconds. The man sprints after it at his best pace, 6 cubits a second. He stays at that pace throughout, but after 30 seconds he will be forced to stop for a minute or two to get his breath back. Will the man catch the goat?

Solution on page 226

PROBLEM 105

T HESE GRIDS MAKE A SEQUENCE, WHERE EACH TAKES ITS APPEARANCE from the one before. What does the fourth grid look like?

1

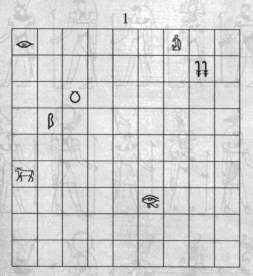

3

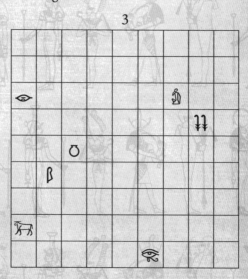

2

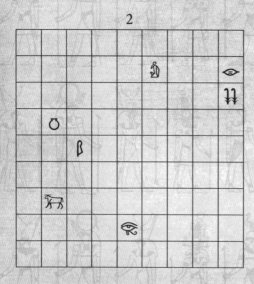

4

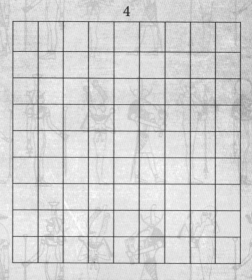

Solution on page 227

PROBLEM 106

AN ARCHER IS ONLY AS GOOD AS HIS LINE OF SIGHT. THIS map identifies the positions of several individuals, but omits a number of obstructions, each taking up an entire square. The number representing each man tells you precisely how many squares he has in his horizontal and vertical lines of sight, including his own. His sight is blocked by obstructions or by the edge of the field, but not by other archers. No two obstructions touch each other horizontally or vertically. Where are they located?

7			6			7			
			2						
					8				5
	9							7	
						8	11		
4			13	9	5				
			8		5	5			7
		13	17						
	12							5	
4			5						
						5			
			17			11			9

Solution on page 228

PROBLEM 107

I N THE ORNAMENTAL GARDENS, TREES AND COLONNADES combine to shade a certain spiral route from the heat of the noon sun. I have taken the liberty of preparing an illustration on this path. If I reveal that each step of the path is 1m in length, how long is the path?

solution on page 228

PROBLEM 108

A PAIR OF MATHEMATICAL OPERATIONS ARE SHOWN HERE, along with their answers. In each case, the digits of the numbers have been replaced, consistently, with symbols. What is the missing number?

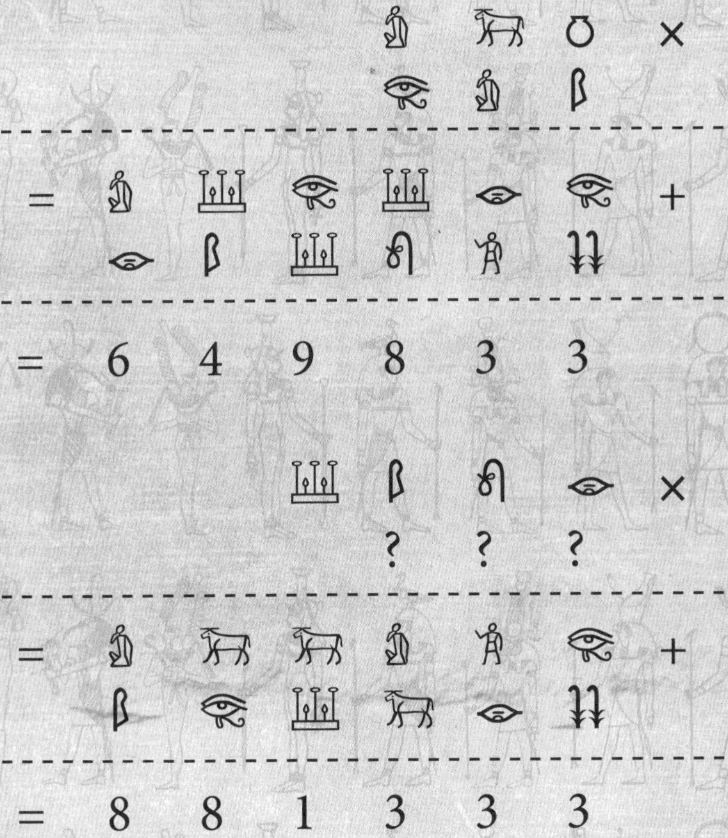

PROBLEM 109

THE MYCENEAN PEOPLE ARE CAPABLE OF A SURPRISING degree of subtlety, if they truly are to thank for this design of distraction. It certainly would go some way to explaining certain of their characteristics. As with other problems of this type, the challenge is to connect the pairs with a single, unbroken line of tiles. The lines move horizontally or vertically, without forming any loops, and without crossing each other. In doing so, they take up the entire grid.

Solution on page 229

PROBLEM 110

I N THIS PROBLEM, THREE PAIRS OF NUMBERS REACH A COMMON solution through different paths of mathematical operation. What is the missing number?

Solution on page 230

PROBLEM 111

◄══◆══►

FOLLOWING A SERIES OF DIRE AUGURIES, A PRIEST OF NEPER
decides that he has to move his grain store a long way, 30
iteru, to the vicinity of Asyut. His camel can carry no more
than 30 1-hekat barrels of grain at any one time, and it needs
to eat one hekat over the course of each iteru it travels, in each
direction. An expensive journey, as well as a lengthy one. The
priest starts with 90 hekats of grain. What is the most that he can
transport to Asyut without sinfully starving his camel?

☥ Solution on page 230 ☥

PROBLEM 112

LABYRINTHS ARE A SCIENCE AS MUCH AS AN ART, AND ONE of the most important elements to bear in mind is that the passages must all interlink. If there is a section that is not accessible, it is not part of the labyrinth.

That truth could be the inspiration for this trial. A space is divided evenly into cells. Each cell is given a numerical value. The task is to remove all duplicated numbers from each horizontal and vertical line of cells, so that only one of each remains. However, this must be done without dividing the remaining cells into two or more groups. It must be possible to navigate between any two cells without hitting a removed spot, moving only horizontally and vertically. Likewise, no two removed spots may be in horizontal or vertical contact. The end result will be a cunning labyrinth indeed.

3	4	11	1	7	5	3	5	6	11
8	8	4	5	10	14	13	14	10	9
10	7	2	6	13	9	9	14	8	8
7	2	3	14	14	4	6	5	2	5
11	5	9	13	4	9	11	10	13	12
3	4	6	4	8	6	5	1	11	7
11	2	1	9	1	8	9	11	12	12
6	7	7	1	9	13	1	8	8	14
9	14	6	8	12	4	10	6	14	4
5	8	10	11	6	5	11	6	1	3
13	6	7	7	11	11	6	12	14	14
5	5	9	14	11	6	12	13	6	1
14	9	12	8	1	2	1	8	13	11
10	3	3	11	10	7	14	11	9	7

Solution on page 231

PROBLEM 113

THE 22 LEADING PRIESTS AND PRIESTESSES OF HATHOR in Upper Egypt met recently in Dendera for a celebratory weekend of feasting. I happen to know that they decided that one of them alone would pay a contribution to the temple to reimburse the High Priestess for the food, drink and entertainments. The matter of who paid was left to the Goddess — the temple servers were instructed to send someone to the table after the final meal, and release every seventh person, counting clockwise, until just one person was left. However, the High Priestess did not tell the servers where to start counting, and one of the priests had been particularly rude during the weekend. So they contrived to ensure that this intemperate priest would be made to pay. If you count the victim as the 1st person in the group, who would the server need to dismiss first?

solution on page 232

PROBLEM 114

THIS PATTERN FOLLOWS A CERTAIN MATHEMATICAL LOGIC.
How many points does the question mark represent?

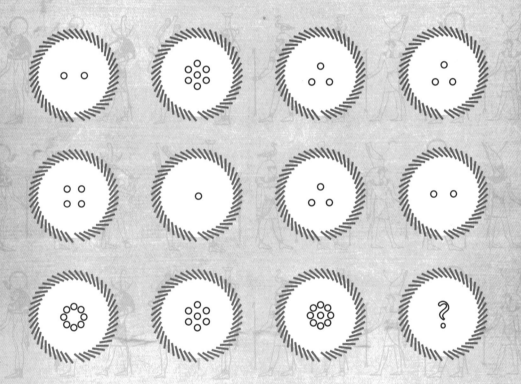

Solution on page 232

PROBLEM 115

❧◆❧

THREE WOMEN WERE RETURNING FROM THE TEMPLE WHEN they found a small pouch of copper deben bits. The first, named Asenath, said, "If I took this, I'd have twice as much as Bithiah." Her friend Bithiah said, "And if I took it, I'd have three times as much as Duathor." Duathor, in turn, said, "Well, if I claimed it, I'd have four times as much as Asenath." Considering least possible whole deben amounts, how much is in the purse, and how much does each woman have?

Solution on page 232

PROBLEM 116

Y OUR CHALLENGE IS TO FIND YOUR WAY FROM THE ENTRANCE at the top of this cunning labyrinth to the exit at the bottom.

Solution on page 233

PROBLEM 117

A REASONABLY SUCCESSFUL MERCHANT HAS DIED, leaving 45 fedw grain barrels to be split evenly between his sons. The fedw hold differing amounts. Nine are full, containing four hekats each. Nine are three-quarters full, holding three hekats. Nine are half-full, with a double-hekat. Nine hold just a single hekat each. Finally, the remaining nine are empty, but an empty hekat-fedw barrel is still of some value. It is clear, totalling the amounts in question, that each son is due to receive 18 hekats of grain, split between nine barrels. However, the barrels are sealed, and the father was a lover of mathematics. He decreed that each son's bequest should be different from those of his brothers, and that each should get at least one of each weight of barrel. The sons beg your indulgence and assistance in deciding how the barrels are to be divided.

Solution on page 234

PROBLEM 118

THE SCALES SHOWN BELOW HERE ARE ALL IN PERFECT balance, as would befit true representations of Ma'at. You may assume that each symbol weighs a whole number of units. What is the least that each may weigh?

Solution on page 234

PROBLEM 119

A LAST SET OF FAKE ICONS OF THE GODS IS DEVOTED TO Anubis, the guardian of the dead. One pair, identical, is genuine, but the other six are clumsily flawed. Which two are the originals?

Solution on page 235

PROBLEM 120

THIS MIGHTY NUMBER SQUARE IS TRULY BLESSED BY
Heka himself. Each row, each column, and each diagonal
line adds up to the same number. The groups of numbers fit into
the empty horizontal spaces in the grid. Can you complete it?

				45				
				73				
				20				
				48				
53	32	64	79	58	12	27	6	38
				5				
				33				
				70				
				17				

9, 15, 21, 35	81, 60, 11, 26
34, 40, 46, 63	49, 24, 43, 78
1, 16, 51, 30	65, 80, 59, 10
29, 44, 76, 55	77, 56, 71, 22
13, 19, 36, 42	24, 3, 18, 50
37, 52, 31, 66	25, 4, 39, 54
62, 68, 74, 7	41, 47, 61, 67
57, 72, 23, 2	69, 75, 8, 14

Solution on page 235

PROBLEM 121

IN ANCIENT KHMUN, IT IS SAID THAT THEY WORSHIPPED EIGHT GODS before learning of the truth of thrice-blessed Thoth. Such a people may well have divided their day into a 16-hour day, 8 of light and 8 of darkness, rather that the 24 we use. It is no great stretch to imagine that each hour could be divided into 64 minutes, and each minute into 64 seconds. A circular time-measuring device for such a people would have 8 hours on its circular face, and 64 lesser divisions. Imagine such a device, at 12 minutes past midday. How many hours, minutes and seconds will it show when its hands next align?

Solution on page 236

PROBLEM 122

H AVING SURVIVED MA'AT'S STERN TEST, THEN JOURNEYED westwards through the Duat, and passed the 21 demon-guarded gates, the fortunate soul joins the eternally living amongst the reed-field islands of Aaru. For each domain, the islands are interconnected by a cunning network of horizontal and vertical paths, sometimes single and sometimes double – in parallel. Each path is as straight as virtue itself, and does not cross any other. In this arrangement of islands, the number of paths touching each one is shown as a number. Given that the islands form one single linked group, where do the paths fall?

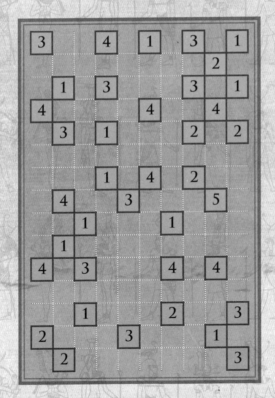

Solution on page 236

PROBLEM 123

T HESE NUMBER GRIDS EACH HAVE THREE SETS OF NUMBERS, which are operated upon in such a way as to produce the letters given as an answer. The underlying logic is identical for each grid. What is the answer to III?

	2	1	6	4				
I	3	3	5	2	C	A	D	B
	5	3	1	2				

	5	3	8	9				
II	3	2	2	3	D	A	D	B
	2	6	6	3				

	9	4	9	4				
III	3	3	2	2				
	3	7	7	6				

solution on page 237

PROBLEM 124

F IVE COOKS RECEIVE THEIR WAGES IN BREAD. THEY HAVE 100 loaves to divide between themselves. They all receive different amounts, but the gap between each share and the next lowest remains equal. The two smallest shares together total just a seventh of the three larger shares. What is the gap?

Solution on page 237

PROBLEM 125

A SUMMARY BOARD NEEDS TO BE PREPARED FROM THESE four game boards. However, a square is only dark on the summary if it is dark on just one of the four boards. In every other instance, it remains uncoloured on the final board. What does the summary board look like?

Solution on page 238

PROBLEM 126

⟡

Various equations are shown here in which the numbers have been replaced with tokens. The answers given are correct, provided that you perform the calculations shown in the order that they are given. What are the numbers?

$$\text{🧎} + \text{🐂} + \text{🦆} + \text{⚱} = 92$$

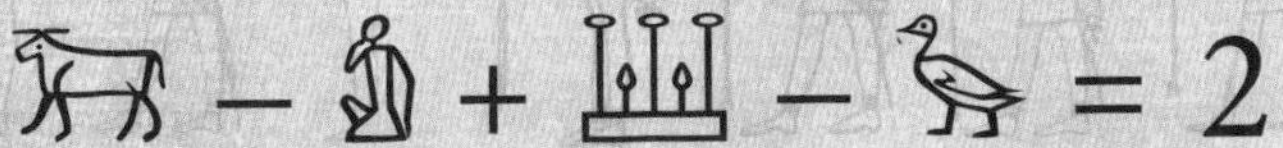

$$\text{🐂} - \text{🧎} + \text{⚱} - \text{🦆} = 2$$

$$\text{🦆} \times \text{🧎} \times \text{🐂} \times \text{⚱} = 228228$$

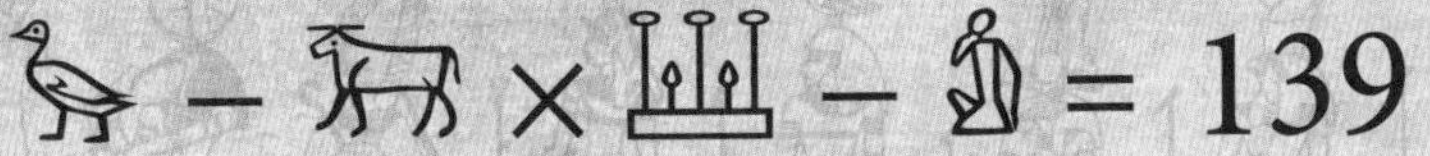

$$\text{🦆} - \text{🐂} \times \text{⚱} - \text{🧎} = 139$$

$$\text{⚱} + \text{🦆} / \text{🧎} \times \text{🐂} = 28$$

⸎ Solution on page 238 ⸎

PROBLEM 127

O N THE SARDESIAN DOCKS, THE MASTER MANAGERS ARE
known for calculating the wiliest of all arrangements of
goods with which to vex their poor workers. As with those of
their lesser colleagues, the grids contain piles of crates. Each pile
holds no less than one crate, and no more than 7. Within the
grid, each row of seven piles contains one pile of each size; the
same holds true for each column. Some piles are guaranteed to
be larger than one or more of their neighbours, and where this is
the case, the restriction is indicated by an arrow.

The grid reproduced here is an example of such a masterwork.
I am certain that it is possible to calculate the precise disposition
of each pile from the information already specified, but it may
require your full attention to complete the grid.

Solution on page 239

PROBLEM 128

THIS IS AN ILLUSTRATION OF THE END OF A CURIOUS game, one whose provenance is unknown to me. An up-arrow ^ is worth eight points. A down-arrow, ∨ is worth six. There are four modifying rules that affect the score.

1. A square that touches the outer double-line grid halves the value of pieces on it.
2. A piece on a blue square earns an extra point.
3. A piece on a yellow square gains an extra third of its value.
4. A piece on a square touching a horizontal black line loses two points.

What is the total value of the pieces on the board?

Solution on page 239

PROBLEM 129

I N THIS GRID, THE SYMBOLS ARE PLACED ACCORDING TO A careful order. Identifying this sequence will allow you to complete the missing section.

Solution on page 240

PROBLEM 130

THIS NUMBER MAZE IS MOST CUNNING. YOU MAY MOVE HORIZONTALLY OR vertically from a square on the top row to a square on the bottom row. Add the value of each square of your route to your total thus far. Going through a square next to a zero — even diagonally — resets your score. However, note that you may only move between numbers and their divisors. Specifically:

2	4	3	5	7	4	3	4	6	3	3	2
6	6	6	2	1	2	3	8	4	6	5	6
8	4	4	3	4	8	2	2	2	8	7	4
1	3	2	6	8	4	7	6	3	2	8	4
2	1	5	4	4	6	1	3	7	1	9	2
5	2	8	6	6	3	5	9	1	5	4	8
4	6	0	6	3	7	4	3	5	2	2	2
9	9	1	9	3	5	8	4	2	1	3	6
7	8	6	1	1	2	9	2	7	3	9	3
2	4	1	2	9	2	8	4	2	6	9	6
6	0	9	3	7	1	2	1	6	5	6	3
5	5	3	5	1	6	3	9	2	0	8	9
2	6	6	7	3	9	5	6	3	6	7	6
4	4	2	8	6	4	4	3	8	8	2	2
9	2	8	8	2	3	9	4	4	1	3	4
1	4	5	1	5	6	2	0	5	3	4	8
3	2	4	2	6	2	6	2	2	9	2	2
6	6	3	3	4	5	4	7	4	2	1	1
5	4	9	6	5	4	3	2	1	4	7	7
8	2	1	5	6	7	5	3	6	7	1	2

From		To
1	-	1, 2, 3, 4, 5, 6, 7, 8, 9
2	-	1, 2, 4, 6, 8
3	-	1, 3, 6, 9
4	-	1, 2, 4, 8
5	-	1, 5
6	-	1, 3, 6
7	-	1, 7
8	-	1, 2, 4, 8
9	-	1, 3, 9

Your task is to find a route that totals 181 points.

Solution on page 241

PROBLEM 131

❧ ⟨ ════◆════ ⟩ ❧

Mirrors deceive, and it is important that the eye be practiced at discerning truth from lies, be they flattery or spiteful rumour. A clouded reflection can cause much harm. These reflections of Tefnut, Lady of Rain, are clouded in just such a way. Just one of the four is true. Which is it?

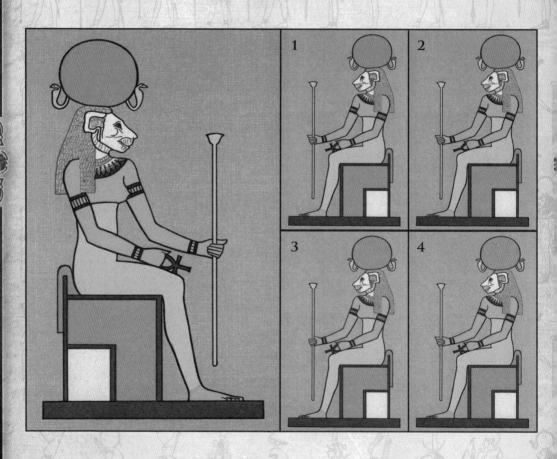

Solution on page 242

PROBLEM 132

— ◆ —

A NUMBER AND ITS 1/7TH PART BECOME 19. WHAT IS IT?

Solution on page 242

PROBLEM 133

T HIS SEQUENCE OF NUMBERS IS PRECISE, BUT CUNNINGLY
contrived. What is the next term?

15   20   20   6   6   19 ?

Solution on page 243

PROBLEM 134

M IGHTY LORD OF THE FORMS OF RE, THERE IS A NUMBER whose digits, added together, total ten. This number divides exactly into every eight-digit number whose first four digits are identical to its second four digits. What is it?

solution on page 243

PROBLEM 135

———◆———

TWO MEN ARE PERFECTLY MATCHED AT THE GAME OF SENET, so much so that each one has an even chance of winning any one game. In order to make a meaningful challenge, they decide to contest a prize by playing a series of an odd number of games. At the end of the series, the one who has won the most games takes the entire prize. Part way into the contest, they are interrupted, and have to cancel. The series is undecided, but one man is in the lead. The man who is winning at that point argues that he should have the prize, as he is doing the best. The man who is losing argues that they should divide the prize equally, as the contest has to be stopped. But there is a fairer option than either of these. What is it?

Solution on page 244

PROBLEM 136

I HAVE FOR YOU HERE AN IMAGE OF SHE WHO FILLS THE Sanctuary With Joy, lovely Hathor to whose kind beauty all women aspire. The four darkened likenesses beside her are all different; just one is the exact duplicate of the Queen of the Dance. Which is it?

✧ Solution on page 244 ✧

PROBLEM 137

A FARMER HAS A GOAT TETHERED TO THE EDGE OF A CIRCULAR field of rushes. He wants it to be able to eat no more than half of the grass. Should the rope used to tether it be longer than, equal to or shorter than the radius of the field?

Solution on page 245

PROBLEM 138

T HIS TABLET HAS BEEN SHATTERED INTO A MULTITUDE of pieces. Given its original appearance and the various elements that make it up, can you see how to reassemble it?

Solution on page 245

PROBLEM 139

———✦———

Ra's battles with Apep have been fierce of late. Without Mehen's coils assisting the sun on his journey, the situation may have become grave indeed. The priests of Ra believe that the tide has turned. They tell me that their efforts have produced this diagram describing Mehen's latest efforts. It is beyond their wit to interpret, even in light of your previous efforts assisting them.

Like previous occasions, they have described a grid. The dotted lines are the spaces which Mehen's body might plausibly occupy. When they have been able to ascertain for certain how many sides of a cell Mehen is lying against, they have recorded that number inside the cell. They are sure that he forms just one gigantic loop. Would you do them the great honour of marking for them where Mehen lies?

3	2	3	2				3	3		3	
	2		2		2						2
2		1					2		3		
2	2	1		1	2	0				1	1
2			3				1	1			
	2		1		1	2	2			2	2
	1	2		2				1	2		
	2	2	2	1			3	2		2	
3			2	3	0			2			
	1		3				3		3		
	2		3	1		3					
2			2	3		3		3	3	3	

Solution on page 246

PROBLEM 140

I SIS, SHE WHO SEEKS JUSTICE FOR THE POOR, IS WELL KNOWN as the lady of magic. Perhaps it is a sign of her enchantment that some differences have arisen between these two depictions of her. There are nine discrepancies in total. Where are they?

Solution on page 247

PROBLEM 141

WITH THE ASSISTANCE OF YOUR PREVIOUS CALCULATIONS, there remains just one worrying encampment on the borders of Punt. As in earlier situations, scouts have been able to tally the number of tents in each row or column of the encampment space, and to locate the trees in there precisely. Each tree is used as support by just one horizontally or vertically adjacent tent. Where are the tents pitched, precisely?

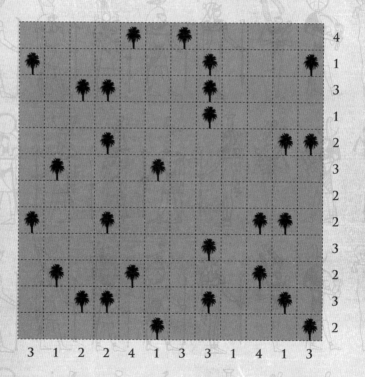

Solution on page 248

PROBLEM 142

IN THIS CHALLENGE, SON OF RE, EACH SYMBOL SHOWN HAS A numeric value. The total of each row and column is reached by summing all of these values. What is each symbol worth?

🐐	𓊖	𓊮	🐐	238
👁	👁	🐐	𓊮	248
𓊖	𓊖🐐	👁	𓊖	270
202	194	180	180	

Solution on page 248

PROBLEM 143

THIS MAGICAL TABLET DIVIDES INTO FOUR IDENTICALLY-shaped, interlocking segments. Each segment contains two of each of the four symbols, as shown. How is it divided?

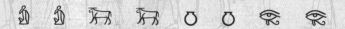

1	2	3	4	5	6	7
	ram	ram		figure	loop	
				figure		
eye		figure		loop		eye
	eye	loop		figure	ram	eye
ram	figure					
	eye			figure		eye
		ram		figure		loop
	loop	figure	loop	ram		eye
		eye			ram	
	loop	loop	ram			

Solution on page 249

PROBLEM 144

GIVEN YOUR MAGNIFICENT EFFORTS ON THE PART OF THE PALACE GUARDS, AND THE increased efforts that have been seen as a result of their ever-swelling love for you, the captain of the guards has suggested that the training barracks might be profitably rearranged. As you may expect, there are a reasonable amount of recruits, many with short service histories, but I am confident that the matter should pose you little trouble. It is a wise man who ensures that those who guard him are perfectly content.

The information supplied shows the space available, and represents each man as the sum of his months of service. Each is to be enclosed in a simple rectangular space, equal in squares to his duration of service. Obviously, no rooms should overlap, and there should be no space left over.

2			24				3	
7		2						2
	7							
							2	
	7							
				4				
				2	8			
2			6	2		11		
							6	
		18		2				9
					3		2	
				2	2			
				3			12	

Solution on page 250

PROBLEM 145

T HERE ARE MANY AND VARIED SYSTEMS OF WRITING numbers. In ours, base ten, '10' means 'one lot of ten'. In base sixty, '10' means 'one lot of sixty'. On that basis, I offer to you two numbers, 748 and 457. One of these two numbers is presented in base 10. The other is not. The two numbers are the same; only the base of their presentation differs. In what base is the other number written?

solution on page 251

PROBLEM 146

T HIS SQUARE OF CLOTH IS A PERFECTLY NORMAL DRAPE. It is of sound construction, woven in the normal manner, less than an arm's width on each side. Yet, without mutilating it or unravelling it, we can place it on the floor and stand on opposite corners, facing each other, and be unable to shake hands. How can this be?

solution on page 251

PROBLEM 147

◆——◆◇◆——◆

THE VISIONS OF MY DREAMS HAUNT ME, TANTALISINGLY beyond my reach, yet encoded into stern numbers. I am close, yet cannot go further. On each line, the numbers convey the sizes of groups of shaded squares. Each group is unbroken, separated from the next by at least one blank space. By comparing horizontal and vertical lines, you may be able to do that which I can not, and recreate the image that has so maddeningly slipped from me.

Row clues (top to bottom):

1.4.1
2.3.3.2
1.2.2.1
1.2.4.2.1
2.1.2.1.2
1.2.2.2.1
1.1.1.1.1
1.1.1.1.1
2.2.1.2.2
1.1.1.1
1.2.2.1
1.1.2.2.1.1
1.1.3.3.1.1
1.2.4.2.1
1.2.2.2.1
2.2.4.2.2
1.2.2.2.2.1
1.10.1
1.3.2.3.1
2.2.2.2.2
1.3.2.3.1
1.4.2.4.1
2.2.6.2.2
1.2.4.2.1

Column clues (left to right, top to bottom):

8 5 4 2 | 4 3 2 2 1 2 1 1 2 1 2 2 3 4 | 2 4 5 8
5 4 4 2 | 4 3 2 4 2 2 1 1 1 2 2 3 3 4 | 2 4 5
4 2 | 1 3 4 4 2 1 2 3 3 2 4 4 1 | 4 5
| 3 3 3 5 7 7 2 3 3 |
| 2 |

PROBLEM 148

I HAVE ONE LAST PROBLEM OF CHAMBERS FOR YOUR amusement. It is a comparatively stern trial, but I remain confident that it will swiftly fall to your incisive analysis. The grid below represents an assortment of interlocked chambers. Each one is made of one or more spaces, connected one to another orthogonally. The number on the tile tells you how many spaces the chamber that encloses it is made of. Chambers of equal size may only touch diagonally. Every space is used. Where are the chambers located?

1				8		5		3	1	2
				6		1				
	1						1	4		1
	7	2	6				4	5	5	
	7	8		1		4	6			5
		1				1				5
1				1					3	1
	1		1	7	7	7	1	3	5	
	6		3							
	1	3						1		
		1		4	1	9	1	3		1

Solution on page 253

PROBLEM 149

IN A HORRIFIC INCIDENT, ONE OF THE DOCK-WORKERS HAS BEEN FOUND BRUTALLY slain. His colleagues are unsavoury, to say the least, and the guard captain who questioned them was foolish enough to speak to them in a group. He came away with set of accusations, counter-accusations and denials, which was all he was able to obtain before the workers, ever clannish, closed ranks and refused to speak further. I know you are just, my Pharaoh, and have no wish to put men to the question. The statements of the men are here, and the guard captain insisted I tell you that he was certain that two of the men were lying. Who is the murderer?

Ikeny: "On the truth of my Ib, the slayer was
Siamun, seized by a maddened rage."

Nehi: "I have not attacked any man or woman.
The assessors know my innocence.
But the dead man was a vile person."

Ankhu: "I will tell you only this: It was not Harkhebi.
He would not harm a dog."

Siamun: "Ikeny is lying to you.
He has always resented me."

Harkhebi: "Nehi always speaks the plain truth.
It is a compulsion for him."

Solution on page 254

PROBLEM 150

THERE ARE A SERIES OF COURTYARDS WITH TOWERS AROUND them. The numbers in the towers are operated upon to result in the number in the courtyard. An identical process is used each time. What is the missing number?

4   3   9   2

$$\boxed{29}$$ $$\boxed{45}$$

5   7   6   6

3   4   8   4

$$\boxed{61}$$ $$\boxed{?}$$

4   5   9   7

Solution on page 255

◆ SOLUTIONS ◆

EASY
SOLUTIONS

SOLUTION 1

4	5	2	6	1	3	7
	v		^			
2	4	3	7	5	1	6
3	1	7	5	6	2	4
			v			
6	2 > 1	4	7	5	3
v	^					
5 > 3	6	2	4	7	1
						^
7	6	5	1	3 < 4	2
		v				
1	7	4	3	2	6	5

167

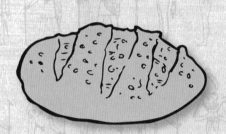

SOLUTION 2

Each man gets 1/3 + 1/5 + 1/15 of a loaf.

SOLUTION 3

No. Once the players understand how the game works,
it will always end in a draw.

―𓂀𓁐𓂀𓋹𓂀𓁐―

SOLUTION 4

10.67m.

―𓂀𓁐𓂀𓋹𓂀𓁐―

SOLUTION 5

The missing value is:
43. 275 × 43=11825 + 36291 = 48116.

SOLUTION 6

SOLUTION 7

60. Multiply the opposing numbers.

SOLUTION 8

The Nile bowmen will make 50 hits, while the chariot
archers will make 48 hits.

SOLUTION 9

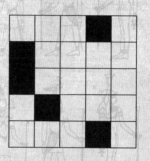

SOLUTION 10

$\text{🧍} = 2$

$\text{🐄} = 3$

$\text{🦆} = 4$

SOLUTION 11

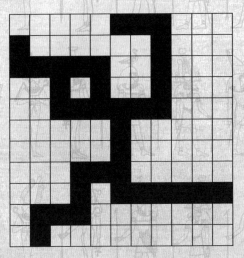

SOLUTION 12

12.

SOLUTION 13

75 cubits.

SOLUTION 14

Each glyph advances 3 squares each time.

SOLUTION 15

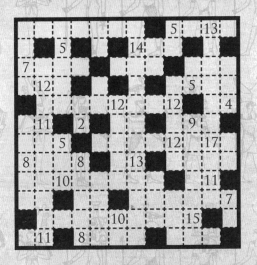

SOLUTION 16

3 and 7.

SOLUTION 17

11	24	7	20	3
4	12	25	8	16
17	5	13	21	9
10	18	1	14	22
23	6	19	2	15

SOLUTION 18

10:45.

SOLUTION 19

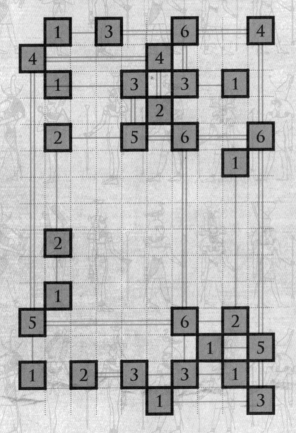

SOLUTION 20

H A E
The three digit number when added to the numbers on
the top two rows gives the number on the bottom row.
So 4765 = 1017 + 2933 + 815. 8 = H, 1 = A and 5 = E.

SOLUTION 21

240 khet an hour.

SOLUTION 22

1	14		5	10		2		12	7
	4	13	3		7	1	5		14
2	13		10	6	9		12	8	4
7	3	14		11	8	6	2	9	
6		5	8	12		10		13	1
	11	1		5	10		6	3	
9	7		11	13		12		5	6
13		8		9	11	7	14	4	
	10	6	2		5		8	1	12
11	8		6	1	3	14	4		13
	12	7		3		4		2	8
12	5		4	14	1	8	7		9
8	9	4		2		3		14	11
5		2	9	7	14		10	11	

SOLUTION 23

Fill 3, put into 5.
Fill 3 from 8, fill 5.
The 8 now holds two, the 5 holds 5, and the 3 holds 1.
Put 5 into 8, then 3 into 5. Fill 3 from 8, and put it into 5.
8 and 5 now both hold four hinu (~2 litres).

SOLUTION 24

0.
Convert the symbols to digits,
and take each row of digits as a number,
and add the numbers.

SOLUTION 25

9.

SOLUTION 26

SOLUTION 27

Rightly or wrongly,
the intent is clear;
if the daughter gets one share,
the mother gets twice that,
and the son gets twice again.
4/7 goes to the son,
2/7 to the mother,
and 1/7 to the daughter.

SOLUTION 28

𓃻	=	4
𓃒	=	5
𓅐	=	7
𓂀	=	1

SOLUTION 29

The sequence is 𓃭𓃾𓊮𓂀𓃭𓃾𓊮𓃀𓃭𓃾𓊮𓃀𓊮𓃀, in a horizontal zig-zag pattern from top left, yielding:

𓂀	𓊮	𓃾
𓂀	𓃭	𓃾
𓊮	𓃀	𓊮

SOLUTION 30

𓃭							𓃭
𓃾	𓊮			𓃾			
					𓂀		𓃀
					𓂀		𓃀
𓊮			𓂀	𓂀			
				𓂀			
𓃾		𓃀	𓃀				
𓃭					𓊮	𓃾	𓃭

183

SOLUTION 31

SOLUTION 32

340.

SOLUTION 33

Bata, by 3.

SOLUTION 34

SOLUTION 35

One route is:

							2		
		6	4	2	0	8	6	4	
		8							
6	4	2	0						
8									
0						8	0	2	
2						6		4	
4	6	8	0	2	4		4	6	8
				6	8	0	2		0
								4	2
				4	2	0	8	6	
		0	8	6					
		2							
	8	6	4						
	0								
	2				8	0	2	4	6
	4				6				8
	6	8	0	2	4				0
					8	6	4	2	
					0				

SOLUTION 36

2.

SOLUTION 37

12.8

SOLUTION 38

21. Each number is equal to the sum of the two before it (starting from 0,1 as givens).

SOLUTION 39

20.

SOLUTION 40

Six cubes for 1 six is likeliest — 66% vs 62% vs 60%.

𒊹 ꝏ ꞎ ☥ ꞏ ꞎ ꝏ 𒊹

SOLUTION 41

2.

𒊹 ꝏ ꞎ ☥ ꞏ ꞎ ꝏ 𒊹

SOLUTION 42

754.

𒊹 ꝏ ꞎ ☥ ꞏ ꞎ ꝏ 𒊹

SOLUTION 43

**Starting from top left and moving row by row
horizontally, you will encounter the pieces in this order:
7. 13. 4. 11. 9. 10. 12. 6. 16. 5. 14. 8. 1. 3. 2. 15.**

SOLUTION 44

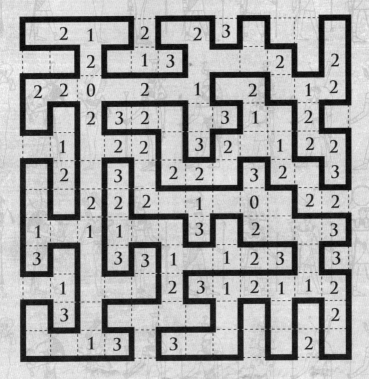

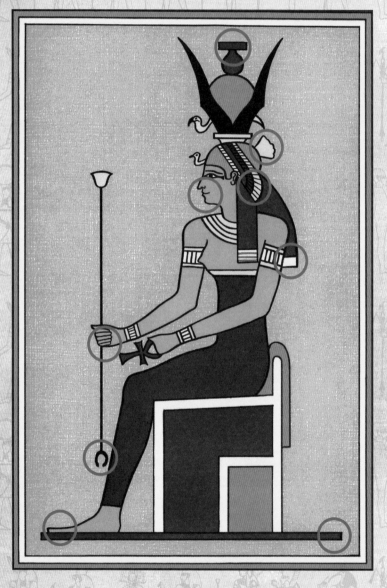

SOLUTION 46

SOLUTION 47

𓀭 = 3. 𓃾 = 2. 𓊝 = 6. 𓂀𓃾 = 5

— 𓀀 𓁿 ☥ 𓁿 𓀀 —

SOLUTION 48

6	6	6	6	1	6	6	6	1	4	4
6	6	1	4	4	1	6	6	6	4	4
9	9	9	4	4	9	9	9	9	9	9
9	9	9	5	5	5	9	9	3	3	1
9	9	9	1	5	5	9	1	3	7	7
1	6	6	6	6	6	1	7	7	7	7
9	9	1	6	1	3	3	1	5	5	7
9	9	6	1	6	6	3	5	5	5	1
9	9	6	6	6	4	4	4	8	8	8
9	9	7	7	7	7	4	2	8	8	8
9	1	7	1	7	7	1	2	1	8	8

SOLUTION 49

55. Only the uncertain can (pessimistically) claim damnation, and the virtuous may not claim false uncertainty. 30 + 15 + 10 = 55.

SOLUTION 50

6+1+4-3 = 8.

MEDIUM
SOLUTIONS

SOLUTION 51

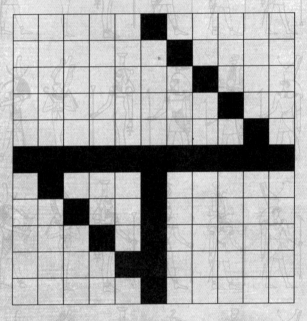

SOLUTION 52

10.25.

SOLUTION 53

 =1. 🐂 =11. 🦆 =9. 👁 =8.

SOLUTION 54

4 and 6.

SOLUTION 55

SOLUTION 56

SOLUTION 57

The first man has 16 debens of copper,
the second has 10, and the third has 6.

SOLUTION 58

1.5625 hekats of grain.
Give yourself a bonus if you thought
to express it with Egyptian fractions,
as $1 + \frac{1}{2} + \frac{1}{16}$.

SOLUTION 59

It will reach its highest point at
the end of 7 days, 4.43 cubits.
It will not escape.

SOLUTION 60

Each glyph moves 1 square to the right, then down as
many squares as the number of the column it moved to.

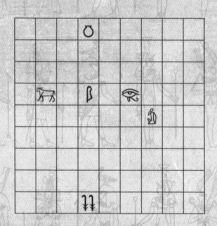

SOLUTION 61

SOLUTION 62

There are just two possible solutions to the matter.
The allocations are either:

2 full, 6 half, and 2 empty;
4 full, 2 half, and 4 empty; and again
4 full, 2 half, and 4 empty,

Or:
4 full, 2 half, and 4 empty;
3 full, 4 half, and 3 empty; and again
3 full, 4 half, and 3 empty.

SOLUTION 63

3	<	5	>	1		6	>	4		2		7
		^										
2		7		5		4		3		6		1
1		3		6	>	5		2		7		4
5		6		2		7		1		4		3
7		1		4	>	2		5	>	3		6
				V								
6		4		3	>	1		7		5		2
4		2		7		3		6		1		5

SOLUTION 64

96.
Each black square is worth the number of its position
on the board (from left to right, with top left being '1').

SOLUTION 65

Calling a collection of things a 'heap'
is a subjective assessment, so there is no
objective answer to when it loses that quality.

SOLUTION 66

4.

＊ ᚥ 𓂀 ☥ 𓂀 ᚦ ＊

SOLUTION 67

9

SOLUTION 68

22	47	16	41	10	35	4
5	23	48	17	42	11	29
30	6	24	49	18	36	12
13	31	7	25	43	19	37
38	14	32	1	26	44	20
21	39	8	33	2	27	45
46	15	40	9	34	3	28

SOLUTION 69

8:43:38.

SOLUTION 70

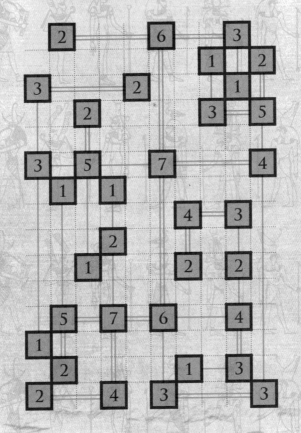

SOLUTION 71

c: F E C. 4939 flipped = 9394.
9394-2741-6000 = 653, F-E-C

SOLUTION 72

18.

SOLUTION 73

The missing value is 27.195 × 27=5265 + 30136 = 35401.

SOLUTION 74

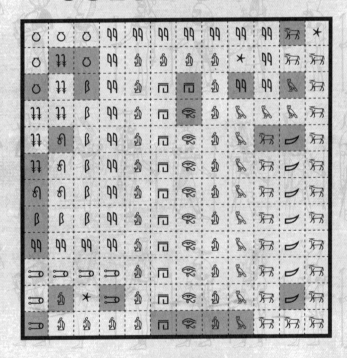

SOLUTION 75

12. Add or subtract the opposing numbers as required.

— 𓀀𓁐𓂀☥𓂀𓁐𓀀 —

SOLUTION 76

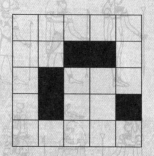

— 𓀀𓁐𓂀☥𓂀𓁐𓀀 —

SOLUTION 77

𓀠 =3. 𓃒 =5. 𓅭 =7. 𓌉 =11.

SOLUTION 78

				8				
					18			
10								
			12					
20								
		26				14		
			28					
					6			
					8			

SOLUTION 79

1392.

—𓀀𓁹𓋹𓁹𓀁—

SOLUTION 80

Two thirds. You are twice as likely to pull a gold kite from the box with two golds in it, so if you already have one gold, that box will show up twice as often as the box with one gold and one silver.

—𓀀𓁹𓋹𓁹𓀁—

SOLUTION 81

3.

—𓀀𓁹𓋹𓁹𓀁—

SOLUTION 82

Just five, weighing 1, 3, 9, 27 and 81 debens. If this seems insufficient, bear in mind that the weights can be added to either or both sides of the balance.

SOLUTION 83

Starting from top left and moving row by row
horizontally, you will encounter the pieces in this order:
13. 7. 10. 6. 14. 12. 16. 3. 15. 9. 8. 1. 11. 5. 4. 2.

SOLUTION 84

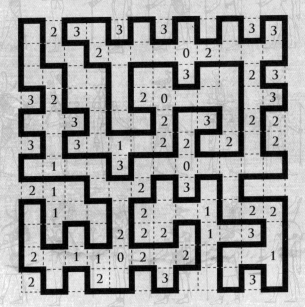

SOLUTION 85

The journey takes the man 2.25 hours, so the dog will run 2.25 iteru (a little over 23.5 km).

SOLUTION 86

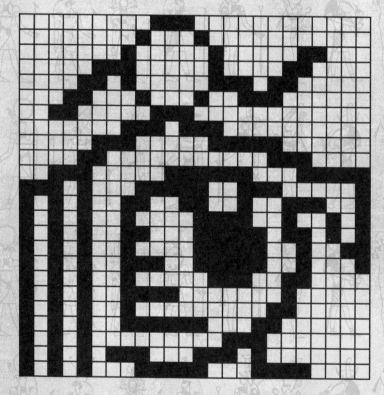

SOLUTION 87

One route is:

SOLUTION 88

Let 'A' be a priest and 'a' his novice:

Aa Bb Cc
Bb Cc > Aa
A Bb Cc < a
ABC > abc
Aa B C < bc
Aa > Bb Cc
Aa Bb < Cc
ab > A B Cc
abc < ABC
a > A Bb Cc
ab < ABCc
> Aa Bb Cc

SOLUTION 89

6		1	8	5		7		11		
9	4	7		3	8	1	14	10	5	
1	3	4	2		14			8	9	
3		8		4	7	10	2	5	14	
	12		4	8		9			7	
11	5	6	1		2	14	9	13	8	
	1	2		13	12		6		4	
12	13		6	2		5	7	14		
10	9	12		14	5	2		4	13	
	7	13	5		10	12	3		2	
5	8		9	12		11		2	6	
8		5	10	9	11		4		7	
2	6	9		7		4	13	12	11	
13		3	7		9	8		1		

SOLUTION 90

One of the fathers was a grandfather,
fishing with his son and grandson. This means that the
other father was both a father and a son, and
there were only three people fishing

SOLUTION 91

2. Convert the symbols to digits,
and take each row of digits as a number,
and subtract the second row from the top row.

SOLUTION 92

The sequence is 🐍🜚🐓🐄👁🝰🐍🐊🜚🐄🐓🝰, in a
clockwise spiral pattern from bottom right, yielding:

SOLUTION 93

36. They are those whole numbers which are spelt out
without using the letter 'e', in ascending order.

SOLUTION 94

47.

—⸗𓆓𓁹☥𓁹𓋴—

SOLUTION 95

SOLUTION 96

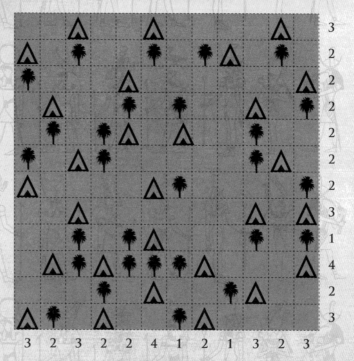

SOLUTION 97

🝓 =5. 🐂 =7. Ⓞ =2. 👁 =1. ß =9

SOLUTION 98

2	1	9	9	9	9	9	7	7	7
2	6	6	9	9	9	9	7	7	1
1	6	6	1	6	6	1	3	1	4
3	3	6	6	7	7	6	3	3	4
3	9	1	7	7	7	1	6	1	4
9	9	9	9	9	7	7	1	6	6
1	9	9	3	1	8	8	6	6	6
3	1	2	1	3	3	8	1	8	1
3	3	2	4	4	4	8	8	1	2
6	6	6	6	4	6	6	3	3	2
1	6	1	6	1	6	1	6	3	1

SOLUTION 99

Ahmes scored 10. Baenre scored 12. Djedhor scored 9.

SOLUTION 100

(20*14) - (12*9) = 172.

223

HARD
SOLUTIONS

SOLUTION 101

Although the two options look the same, in fact they are completely different situations, and cannot be compared in this way. The issue is an illusion. In either direction, the average worth is 150% of the lower value.

SOLUTION 102

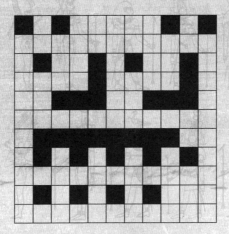

SOLUTION 103

265.

SOLUTION 104

Yes. He will catch the goat on the 30th second,
at a total distance of 177 cubits.

SOLUTION 105

Each glyph moves 1 square down then 1 square to the left if it ends on an even numbered row, or 1 square to the right if the row is odd numbered.

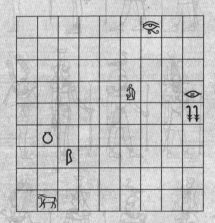

SOLUTION 106

7		6		■			7	■	
	■	2	■						■
		■				8			5
■	9	■		■			■	7	
						■	8	11	
4	■	13		9		5	■		
			8	■	5	■	5		7
■	13	17						■	
	12		■		■			5	■
4	■		5	■			■		■
	■					■	5		
	■	17				11			9

SOLUTION 107

82m.

SOLUTION 108

The missing value is:

$$364.1372 \times 364 = 499408 + 381925 = 881333$$

— ⸗𓂀𓋹𓆣 —

SOLUTION 109

SOLUTION 110

36. Reach the common number through adding,
multiplying or raising one number
to the power of the other.

$$= \mathrel{?}\mathord{?}\mathord{?}\mathord{?}\mathord{?} =$$

SOLUTION 111

15 hekats. In the first journey, the camel takes 30,
leaves 15 at a dump 7.5 iteru (~80km) away, and
returns with nothing, having eaten the other 15.
In the second journey, the camel again takes 30.
At the 7.5 iteru dump, it replenishes the grain it
has eaten, and goes on to the half-way mark,
the 15 iteru point. It drops off the 7.5 hekats of
grain it just picked up, and then returns directly,
finishing its 30-hekat original load to arrive back
once more with nothing. Finally, the camel collects
the last 30 hekats and sets off again. At the first dump,
it collects the remaining 7.5 hekats, replacing
what it has eaten so far. At the midway dump, it
again picks up the 7.5 hekats it left last time, again
topping it back up to a full load. Finally, it travels the
remaining 15 iteru to Asyut, leaving the priest with just
15 hekats of grain — but truly, a happy God is priceless.

SOLUTION 112

	4	11	1	7		3	5	6	
8		4	5		14	13		10	9
10	7	2	6	13		9	14		8
7		3		14	4	6		2	5
11	5		13	4	9		10		12
3		6	4	8		5	1	11	7
	2	1	9		8		11	12	
6		7		9	13	1		8	14
9	14		8	12		10	6		4
	8	10		6	5	11		1	3
13	6		7		11		12	14	
5		9	14	11	6	12	13		1
14	9	12		1	2		8	13	11
	3		11	10	7	14		9	

SOLUTION 113

If the victim is in position 1, start with position 7. There is no hard and fast rule for this type of question, but pick a number at random and see where it takes you, and that will give you the offset between first and last.

SOLUTION 114

6. Convert the symbols to digits and multiply each top-row number individually with the one directly beneath it to give the one on the bottom row.

SOLUTION 115

The purse holds 23 deben. Asenath has 9, Bithiah has 16 and Duathor has 13.

SOLUTION 116

SOLUTION 117

It is easiest to specify each barrel as its weight in grain.
One son has to get: 4+4+4+3+2+1+0+0+0
Then there are three possible pairs of bequests, and
any two of those three pairs will solve the dilemma.
These are:
4+3+3+3+2+2+1+0+0 and 4+4+3+2+2+1+1+1+0;
4+3+3+3+2+1+1+1+0 and 4+4+3+2+2+2+1+0+0; and
4+3+3+2+2+2+1+1+0 and 4+4+3+3+2+1+1+0+0.

SOLUTION 118

🜂 =3. 🐐 =1. 𐦼 =6. 𓂀 =8. β =2. 𐦀 =4.

SOLUTION 119

1 and 3.

— 𓄿𓂀𓋹𓂀𓆓 —

SOLUTION 120

1	16	51	30	45	77	56	71	22
41	47	61	67	73	9	15	21	35
69	75	8	14	20	34	40	46	63
13	19	36	42	48	62	68	74	7
53	32	64	79	58	12	27	6	38
81	60	11	26	5	37	52	31	66
25	4	39	54	33	65	80	59	10
29	44	76	55	70	24	3	18	50
57	72	23	2	17	49	24	43	78

SOLUTION 121

1:09:09.

= ⟨ 𓂀 ☥ 𓂀 𓀛 =

SOLUTION 122

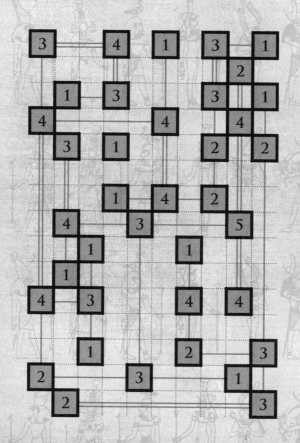

SOLUTION 123

B C D C

Each bottom row number is determined by the two numbers above it. The letters represent the functions used in each column (addition, subtraction, multiplication or division).

Column 1: $9 \div 3 = 3$ ÷ is B

Column 2: $4 + 3 = 7$ + is C

Column 3: $9 - 2 = 7$ - is D

Column 4: $4 + 2 = 6$ ÷ is C

SOLUTION 124

9.167 (or 9 + 1/6).

SOLUTION 125

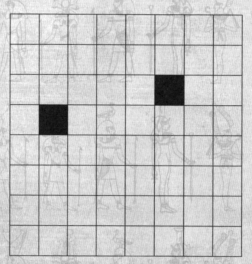

SOLUTION 126

𒀭=26. 🐃=14. 🦢=19. 𓏥=33.

SOLUTION 127

7	3	6	4 < 5	1	2
1	7	5	3	6	2	4
5	4 > 2	1 < 3	7	6
3	5 < 7	6	2	4	1
2 > 1	3 < 5	4	6	7
6	2	4	7	1	3	5
4	6	1	2	7	5 > 3

SOLUTION 128

48.

SOLUTION 129

The sequence is

𓃮𓏲 𓃮𓏲 𓄿𓏲 𓄿𓏲 𓄿𓏲 𓃮𓏲,

in an anticlockwise spiral pattern from top left, yielding:

🐏	ß	ß
𓂀	♌	♌
♌	𓂀	🐏

SOLUTION 130

One route is:

			7							
			1							
			4	8	2	2				
						6		2	8	4
						3		1		2
						9	1	5		8
										2
										6
								3	9	3
				2	8	4	2	6		
			7	1						
			1							
			3							
			6							
2	8	8	2							
4										
2										
6	3									
	9									
	1									

SOLUTION 131

1.

= 𓃀𓁹𓋹𓁹𓃀 =

SOLUTION 132

16.625 (or 16 + ½ + ⅛,
if you want to be accurately Egyptian about it.)

SOLUTION 133

19. The numbers indicate the position in the alphabet of first letter of each of the natural numbers when written out — (O)ne, (T)wo, (T)hree, and so on.

SOLUTION 134

73.

SOLUTION 135

The best answer is, taking the current score
at a starting point, to work out the probability
of each man proving the victor by the end of the series.
What you have that, divide the prize between the two
men according to each one's likelihood of winning.
So if the man who is currently losing has a 40% chance
of reaching victory, he gets two fifths of the money.

SOLUTION 136

4.

SOLUTION 137

Longer — 1.16 times the radius, to be exact.

SOLUTION 138

Starting from top left and
moving row by row horizontally,
you will encounter the pieces in this order:
9. 29. 10. 15. 22. 19. 6. 14. 21. 2. 25. 12.
8. 20. 16. 3. 26. 4. 28. 18. 7. 11.
24. 5. 13. 17. 1. 27. 23.

SOLUTION 139

SOLUTION 140

SOLUTION 141

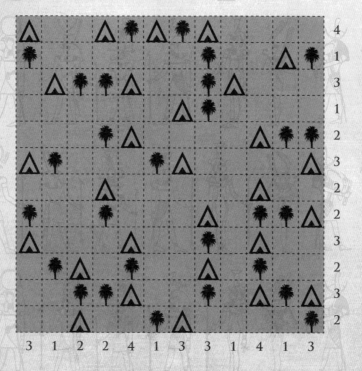

SOLUTION 142

 =27. =31. =29. =35. =37.

SOLUTION 143

SOLUTION 144

2			24				3	
7		2						2
	7							
							2	
		7						
					4			
				2		8		
2			6	2		11		
							6	
		18		2				9
					3		2	
				2	2			
				3			12	

SOLUTION 145

748 is in base 10. 457 is in base 13.

SOLUTION 146

This may happen if I place
the cloth under a closed door,
and we stand either side.

SOLUTION 147

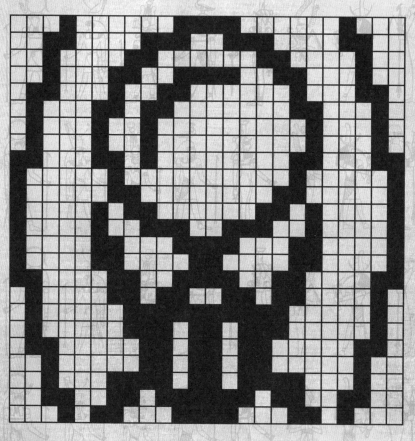

SOLUTION 148

1	8	8	8	8	5	5	3	3	1	2
8	8	8	8	6	5	1	3	4	4	2
7	1	2	6	6	5	5	1	4	4	1
7	7	2	6	6	6	4	4	5	5	5
7	7	8	8	1	4	4	6	6	6	5
7	7	1	8	8	7	1	6	6	6	5
1	8	8	8	1	7	7	7	3	3	1
6	1	8	1	7	7	7	1	3	5	5
6	6	3	3	9	9	9	9	9	5	5
6	1	3	4	4	9	9	9	1	3	5
6	6	1	4	4	1	9	1	3	3	1

SOLUTION 149

If exactly two statements are false, the
only self-consistent possibility is
that the murderer is Harkhebi,
and the liars are Ikeny and Ankhu.